NATIONAL GEOGRAPHIC DIRECTIONS

The Mays of Ventadorn

ALSO BY W. S. MERWIN

Poetry:
The Pupil
A Mask for Janus
The Dancing Bears
Green with Beasts
The Drunk in the Furnace
(Editor) West Wind: Supplement of American Poetry
The Moving Target
Collected Poems
The Lice
Animae
The Carrier of Ladders
(With A. D. Moore) Signs
Asian Figures
Writings to an Unfinished Accompaniment
The First Four Books of Poems
The Compass Flower
Feathers from the Hill
Finding the Islands
Opening the Hand
The Rain in the Trees: Poems

W. S. MERWIN

The Mays of Ventadorn

NATIONAL GEOGRAPHIC DIRECTIONS

NATIONAL GEOGRAPHIC
Washington D.C.

Published by the National Geographic Society
1145 17th Street, N.W., Washington, D.C. 20036-4688

Text copyright © 2002 W. S. Merwin
Map copyright © 2002 National Geographic Society

Rebec on cover courtesy of Paul Butler

Library of Congress Cataloging-in-Publication Data

    Merwin, W. S. (William Stanley), 1927-
    The Mays of Ventadorn/W.S. Merwin.
    p. cm. – (National Geographic directions)
    ISBN 0-7922-6538-6
    1. Limousin (France)–Description and travel. 2. Merwin, W. S. (William Stanley),
    1927—Journeys–France–Limousin. 3. Troubadours. 4. Bernart, de Ventadorn, 12th
    cent. 5. Château de Ventadour Site (France) I. National Geographic Society (U.S.) II.
    Title. III. Series.

    DC611.L732 M47 2002
    818'.5403–dc21

                      2002019348

Book design by Michael Ian Kaye and Tuan Ching, Ogilvy & Mather, Brand Integration Group

Printed in the U.S.A

To Margaret MacElderry

CONTENTS

The Mays of Ventadorn

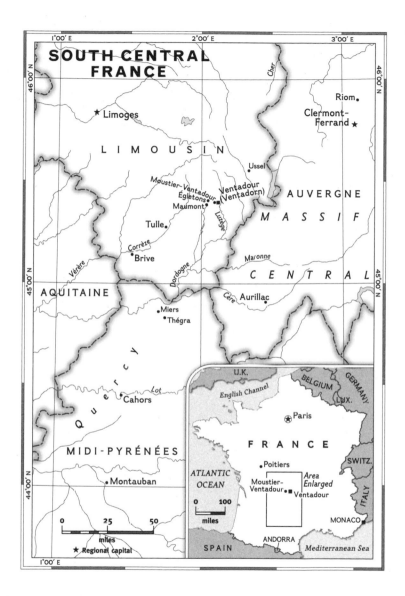

SOUTH CENTRAL FRANCE

1°00' E   2°00' E   3°00' E

46°00' N

★ Limoges

Riom.

Clermont-
Ferrand ★

L I M O U S I N

Ussel

Moustier-Ventadour
Églétons•
Maumont•

Ventadour
(Ventadorn)

A U V E R G N E

Tulle.

Luzège

M A S S I F

Corrèze
• Brive

Dordogne

Maronne

Vézère

C E N T R A L

45°00' N

A Q U I T A I N E

Cère

Aurillac

• Miers
• Thégra

Q u e r c y

Lot

• Cahors

M I D I - P Y R É N É E S

44°00' N

• Montauban

```
0       25      50
|___|___|___|___|___|
        miles
★ Regional capital
```

1°00' E

Inset map:

U.K.

English Channel

BELGIUM

GERMANY

LUX.

⊛ Paris

F R A N C E

• Poitiers

SWITZ.

Moustier-
Ventadour• Ventadour

Area
Enlarged

ATLANTIC
OCEAN

```
0       100
|___|___|
  miles
```

ITALY

MONACO

SPAIN

ANDORRA

Mediterranean Sea

CHAPTER ONE

In the light between rains on a morning late in spring, the wooded hillsides, the squat stone farmhouses, the barnyards, and the tall, shell-gray, isolated ruins on the ridge appeared to be standing in a single shadow.

The ruins were all that was left, by the end of the twentieth century, of the château of Ventadour (or, in its original Occitan, Ventadorn) in the volcanic foothills of the Massif Central, in southern France. In its youth, early in the twelfth century, the château had been the home of Bernart de Ventadorn, one of the greatest of the troubadours.

Most of the older pictures of the ruins and of the nearby village appear to have been taken in winter. The trees, from a time just before ours, stand like cracks in the walls, and all the colors are depths of sepia, or black and white washed to gray. The human figures, whose originals had long since departed by the time I saw their likenesses, stare at the then-visible camera with fixed disbelief, far away in the knowledge that the picture of them, even as it is being taken, belongs to another life, and that they will never see that glass eye again. And in fact their pictures, and odds and ends of their lives and of the light around them at those moments, turn up years later in attics and old bookstores and are pored over by strangers who do not know who they are or were and will never know anything more about them. The bare limbs of the big trees reaching over them, and over the roofs, have been taken away during the time between us, and some of the roofs and walls too, so that the place itself, in a period no greater than a couple of generations (traversed by one war, out of earshot, or perhaps two), has become all but unrecognizable, dark against its grainy sky.

But when I recall the ruins and the country around them, almost always from somewhere else, often from another part of the world and of the calendar, I am sure to see them, at least to begin with, as I did the first time I approached them, in the cool, veiled light of spring, the new leaves fully open, shining with rain, the white stars of stitchwort and blackberry, and the brilliant yellow gorse and broom flowers shining against the rough, mossy walls along the lanes, their colors glowing in the overcast daylight.

I was not thinking then, as I have since, of how long I had been on my way to that glimpse of the jagged shards of ramparts and towers standing by themselves on their steep hilltop, and so I did not recall that it had been in the spring, too, that I had taken one of the first definite steps toward them, though I had no idea of that at the time. It was in Washington, D.C., at

Easter, during one of my last years as a student. I was visiting a college friend in the city, and while I was there I telephoned St. Elizabeth's Hospital, and to my surprise learned that I would be allowed to call on Ezra Pound and that he was willing to see me.

On a morning of bright sunlight, one of the first warm days of spring, I took the bus across Washington to the hospital. I had with me not the worn volume of Pound's own *Personae* with its spare stick-portrait of Pound by Gaudier-Breszka on the rough-textured yellow jacket—at the time that would have seemed to me embarrassingly obvious. Instead I was carrying John Peale Bishop's *Collected Poems*. In it, the few pages of his little-known but superb translations included two versions of poems by troubadours, one by Bertran de Born, and one of Jaufre Rudel's most famous songs, about a love for someone far away, in the spring. I realize now that Bernart de Ventadorn must have known Jaufre Rudel's poem by heart in his youth, from having heard it sung at Ventadorn, and its theme is woven through all his own poems and what we can deduce, however dubiously, of his life. The title, which (when the poem was printed) was the first line, *Quan Lo Rius De La Fontana,* gave me the first words of Provençal (or, as we have come to call it, Occitan) that I had heard, or imagined I had heard. The translation was, after all, a translation, but it brought a suggestion of the whole tradition, which seemed like an invitation.

When the thin fountains are again
Clear streams and sunlight interfused,
When flower of the wild rose is seen,
And nightingales upon the bough

Smooth and renew with changed refrain
Their sweet songs, I too must begin
Sweetly to rearrange my own.

It is a little fancy for Rudel, whose haunting elegance is made of language so simple that Rudel's *vida,* composed a century or more after he lived, says his poems had fine music and *paubres mots*—poor, or perhaps merely plain or ordinary, words.

I knew Pound's own strange, roughened pre-Raphaelite, archaized versions of Bertran de Born, and Dante's portrayal of that poet in the *Inferno* among the sowers of discord, holding his severed head up in front of him like a lantern. But it was not, in fact, the Provençal poems that I was mulling over as the bus rolled along past the National Gallery, under the new translucent leaves. *Personae* contained Pound's *Homage to Sextus Propertius,* which I knew more or less by heart, and I was returning with pleasure to Bishop's brief translation from the Latin of Petronius Arbiter—"Can it indeed be, Jove, you have grown old?"—something that Bishop had done, along with the two troubadour translations, in 1933, when he was forty-one. An age that was then altogether too remote to imagine. A girl standing beside me on the crowded bus noticed what I was reading. I caught her eye and she said how much she loved poetry, and how little encouragement there was for her to find a place for it in her present life and work. This was her first year in Washington, she said. Government. Good job. Oh yes. "Sometimes—," she said, and shrugged, using the word "sordid." Dark bangs across her forehead. Very pretty. She got off at the next stop, just past the museum.

The hospital at that time was a collection of large nine-teenth-century brick buildings. They appeared to have been built in the years after the Civil War, with fire escapes and portico roofs probably added later. They looked hard-worn and tired, but the stains and cracks running down the brickwork, as I recall the place, may be imaginary touches supplied more recently, in remembering it. The building to which my inquiries led resembled a big down-at-heels municipal school—a larger, broader, duller version of the brick neo-Gothic Abraham Lincoln School #14, between Academy and Division Streets in Scranton, Pennsylvania, which I attended for five years of my childhood. A dingy entrance, and at the top of a flight of stairs an attendant opened a heavy, metal-covered door, and I found myself in a large, ill-lit, sparsely furnished public room, its walls a wan, glaucous green. A facility. Quite obviously something that was thought of as a necessary evil.

Pound was led down an inner flight of steps that looked like the bottom of a circling staircase in a tower, and he welcomed me, when the attendant stepped aside, with an openmouthed smile, his head thrown back. We sat down in an alcove, in two veteran easy chairs. The distance between us was beyond calculation. Small-voiced good will calling across a canyon. He began to talk to me as though I knew many things whose very names I had never heard, and I nodded and murmured as appropriately as possible.

The *Pisan Cantos* had been published fairly recently. I knew something of their story, and something, mostly hearsay, of the government's case against Pound, but I had read next to nothing about his politics and did not know what to make of the things

I had heard. I understood that the insanity plea had perhaps saved his life, and the most frequent question I heard about Pound at the time was whether or not he was crazy. I had not read his statements about fascism or his anti-Semitic rantings. I did not want to believe some of the things I had heard about him, and certainly I did not want him to be shot, which at the time was said to be—or at least to have been—quite possible. Looking back, I am surprised to realize how easily I was able to focus my enthusiasm on the poetry alone, and on what I regarded as Pound's intransigent, undeflected devotion to it. I admired him for passages in his poems, some of which still seem to me new and gemlike. The startling vitality of those lines allowed me to cling to something that I thought exemplary in him: He was an American—middle-class and in every sense provincial, as I was—who had set out from the beginning to be an artist, a poet. And to do it without money. I felt that I was already in his debt, and at that age I did not want to hear things about him that I would not be able to come to terms with.

He talked about Confucius, kept returning to him. And about Bill Williams, with approval but as though he were remembering another time. Pound then was in his sixties, but to me he seemed like an ancient, and when he looked back it must have seemed to him that he had lived through several distinct lives. He talked about *The Cantos,* his cantos, and about that magic trick that he predicted so many times: When the hundredth canto was finished, he said (demonstrating with his hands in the air), the capstone would fit perfectly across the columns of the temple and everything would be seen to be in place. I was eager to ask him the right things, but for the most part he took care of all that. He was glad to have someone who wanted to listen to him.

Behind him a man in pajamas wandered up and down the long room looking at the high discolored ceiling, pausing to reach up and pull some invisible object—a chain, a rope—and listen. Flushing toilets. The door opened and an attractive, elegant woman, of an age between Pound's and mine, was let in to visit him, bringing a large bouquet of mimosas. Affectionate greetings, embraces, kisses. It seemed to me a glimpse of Europe, of the great world. He introduced her to me, muttering her name—European, multisyllabic—so fast that I caught nothing. I made a move to leave but he said to stay. The visiting hours would not be over for some time yet. His friend said she was not staying anyway. She said she came by often, and would have longer tomorrow. I walked to the window for a moment while they talked. As I remember there were wires, like chicken wire, embedded in the glass, and a heavy metal screen outside it, which contributed to the dinginess of the light in the room. When I turned back she was preparing to go, and I never learned who she was.

He went back to talking—about Cocteau now, whose poems he liked, and it was not easy for him to find contemporary poets he wanted to read. He spoke in the key of judgment the greater part of the time. He talked about reading in general. "Have you noticed," he asked, "that senators never read the newspapers?" I admitted that I had never noticed that. "That," he explained confidentially, "is because a political party goes to pot when it begins to believe its own lies." I hoped he would veer back to the subject of poetry, and he did, and talked about Eliot. Tom. But again a distance, a remoteness, seemed to hover around his words. I wanted to ask him about Yeats, but he took me by surprise and turned the subject to me, or someone he took to be me. Someone, as he seemed quite prepared to believe, who was bent on spending his life trying to write poetry. He had been lucky, he said, to have known a generation of writers who had never thought of writing for money. He told me he imagined I was serious, and that if I was I should learn languages, "so as not to be at the mercy of translators." And then I should translate, myself. "If you're going to be a poet," he said, "you have to work at it every day. You should write about seventy-five lines a day. But at your age you don't have anything to write about. You may think you do, but you don't. So get to work translating. The Provençal is the real source. The poets are closest to music. They hear it. They write to it. Try to learn the Provençal, at least some of it, if you can. Meanwhile, the others. Spanish is all right. The *Romancero* is what you want there. Get as close to the original as you can. It will make you use your English and find out what you can do with it."

When the visiting hour was nearly over, his wife, Dorothy Shakespear, arrived. A tall, quiet, gentle Englishwoman whom I liked immediately, and Pound turned me over to her, speaking of me as though we had known each other for some time and I were a literary person of established consequence. Then the attendant came and led Pound away and up the inner staircase, where the light appeared to be better, and Dorothy and I were led out through the doorway to the world at large.

She invited me to tea, to meet their son Omar, who lived with her a few blocks from the hospital. Their apartment was on the top floor of an old house. One wall of the small, long living room sloped under the roof. Garret windows, looking out through trees over Washington, stood open to the spring afternoon. I wondered whether that view of the city through the upper branches would remind her of Europe, which I had never seen, or whether it looked completely foreign to her. A lute was hanging on a yellow wall. This was the literary world. Another plane of existence, intelligent and mature. This was a detail of a vast domain, so far known only by hearsay. That reserved, kind, modest woman had known Yeats well, and Eliot, and Joyce, and Wyndham Lewis, and many of their generation and of their elders in London and Paris and Italy, and had listened to their views through the years between the wars. I wanted to ask her everything and realized that I did not know where to begin, and I asked her next to nothing. A little about her life in Washington, in an undirected way. She showed me some late periodical publications of pieces by Yeats, which she had there for some reason that was not clear to me.

Omar came in, a thin, quick, nervous young man of my own age, with a hurried English way of talking. The family joke was that Ezra had wanted him to be called Omar to make sure that he would never be a poet. Omar, and then both of them, began to talk about the war, the blitz in London where they had been together, and Omar described his anxious dread, ever since, even across the Atlantic in an American city, of any loud noise. He talked of sleeping under tables, listening to the planes and the bombs, and he said that he still woke up very often thinking that he was there and the raids were going on.

Before I left, Dorothy gave me a copy of Pound's newly published *The Unwobbling Pivot,* translated from Confucius. And Pound's own kindness persisted, along with evidence of his unchecked love of giving advice. Not long after the visit, he sent me, via Omar, a copy of *A Draft of XXX Cantos,* inscribed to me in pencil (I wonder whether he was allowed to have a pen— I think it was Theodore Spencer who took him a portable typewriter), and we managed to maintain a flurry of correspondence for a while. He sent me bits of gnomic instruction on postcards, always scrawled in pencil, the handwriting clearly reflecting his quick impulsiveness. The most memorable of them read, in full, "Read seeds not twigs EP."

His persistent urging to return to sources, the points where things began—or what, in retrospect, appear to have been such points: moments of emergence when something quite new suddenly seemed possible—ran through his essays, which no doubt he had assumed I knew word for word. After the meeting I returned to them searching, as I now realize, through their tone of irritated, autocratic pedagogy, for the notes that rang true and might be real guides. "A return to origins," he had written in the essay *The Tradition,* "invigorates because it is a return to nature and reason. The man who returns to origins does so because he wishes to behave in the eternally sensible manner." Reading the words now I hear, I think, what attracted him in Confucius, the gnostic leap without concern for logic, a tone like that of the text of Wilhelm's translation of the *I Ching.* But at the time it seemed clear to me that he was talking about a craving for the presence of authenticity in the relation between words and experience, and a way of edging closer to the recognition of it.

Yet when I returned to Pound's own representations in English of the troubadour songs, and of the troubadours' near-contemporary thumbnail biographies, they seemed, as they had before, to be couched in a language that no one could have spoken or sung in any age, a jangling, affected concoction of neo-Gothicisms, a mannerism dreamed up for a high-school production of *Ivanhoe*. "and he delighted himself in chançons, to learn and to make them...And he fell in love with the wife of the Count, in the form of pleasure...Worth lieth riven and Youth dolorous..." I was not happy to admit how I felt about this sort of fustian from the poet who kept insisting that others should "make it new." How appropriate could these pasteboard archaisms be in representing survivals of a tradition at its inception, when presumably it had no antiquated usages to resort to? I may have failed to notice some of the moments when the power of the original broke through the distances and could be heard in Pound's English, as in these lines from Peire Cardenal (Pound spells his name Cardinal, I do not know why):

As a man weeps for his son or for his father,
Or for his friend when death has taken him,
So do I mourn for the living who do their own ill...

Even then I had come to suspect that Pound's words, in his poems and his discursive writings, would always matter to me most as fragments.

I was familiar with only a few words and phrases of "the Provençal" then, but I had been trying to learn Spanish for a few years, and I got the *Romancero* out of the college library. I leafed through it, I am sure, at random, and the first poem I paused at and tried to haul into some sort of life in English began with the line *"Descolorida zagala."* I thought there had to be a way of conveying that in English. I had not taken into consideration that those two words might not comprise a particularly vibrant bit of poetry in the original. *Descolorida*—what magic could give the proper sense and grace to that? "Pale maiden" of course would simply be wan, voiceless and dull. I had not learned what must be one of the first things: where to start, what poem or line might be worth trying to move across the silence between languages. A few weeks after I got back from Washington I managed to get a copy of Hill and Bergin's *Anthology of the Provençal Troubadours*. I hunted for trots in the library and scribbled in the margins of my book, and then proceeded to approach the words as raw material and see whether somehow they could be coaxed into producing a live sound that might bear a resemblance to the life of the original. For a long time nothing at all seemed to come to life in English.

I was not a gifted or even an assiduous linguist. Years of Spanish had not yet enabled me to converse readily in the language or to follow with the sensitive comprehension they deserved Americo Castro's brilliant graduate lectures on Cervantes's *Novelas Ejemplares*. I had squeaked into graduate school in Romance languages on the basis of schoolbook Spanish and what French I had managed to acquire in one summer, taking crash courses at McGill University in Montreal, and since there was no one who could provide a course in Provençal—as everyone called the language then—I signed up for Old French as the nearest thing I could get to it, ignorant at the time of the bitter historic ironies in the substitution.

Our professor was a French medievalist, stooped, hollow-cheeked, gray-skinned, emaciated, barely audible. To our youth he appeared to have arrived from a Daumier drawing by a process of dehydration. He gave the impression at all times of being the embodiment of his archaic subject, with nothing left over to be a person. There were never more than three or four students. One was a huge Russian whose passions were chess and Rabelais—an author whom I suspected of having influenced his stories about himself and his family.

We sat in a tower of the old library building, a long room among the rafters, a kind of loft that had never been finished like the rooms on the floors below, so that our graceless attempts at giving voice to a few sounds and phrases of medieval French took place inside masonry that had been designed to resemble a fortified belfry or a keep with battlements. The dusty boards and beams, the bare stones, gave the old attic an air of being akin to all sorts of other places—the backstage of a theater, the balcony of a church, a barn, or (if one had never seen a castle) a castle. None of us, I suspect, would have admitted that the setting was appropriate. We were at an age, and it was a time, when nineteenth century academic and ecclesiastical neo-Gothic architecture was about as fashionable as Poe's *Ulalume*. I was aware that the style of the building had been imitated from Anglo-Norman originals, some of them vaguely familiar from steel engravings encountered in childhood. I even knew the dates of a few of those ancient structures, but I scarcely believed they had ever existed. The age from which the building in which we studied entered my awareness was the shadowy unnumbered past of grandparents and great-grandparents who had not kept track even of their own unquestioned certainties, and in whose lost memories the origins of the present lay in darkness. So neither the period of the historic models nor the one that had given rise to the actual tower where we sat over unresponsive words was altogether credible or immediate to us, as we groped to conjure up some sense of a language that had been obsolete for four hundred years.

In fact, the architecture of the Anglo-Norman originals of the tower had evolved during the generations just after Archambaud Rotten-Leg, also known as Archambaud the Butcher, earned his names, however and wherever he did, and after his son, Viscount Eble II, supervised the raising of the first ramparts on the hilltop at Ventadorn, some time between the horrors of the Norman conquest of England and those of the First Crusade. But it would be many years before those connections occurred to me.

The Old French was stiff and strange in sound and spirit, but it brought me a step closer to the poetry of François Villon—not part of the intention of the course—for which I remain grateful. And it led me to one poem that, while it was not actually in "the Provençal," was in every other respect a representation of the troubadour tradition in its prime. It was the famous *Chanson* of Richard I of England, a poem with a legend of its own, a story of the kind of which operas have been made. I knew virtually nothing of that story when I worked on the translation, and certainly it was worth knowing. This is how the poem came to be written, as far as is known.

Richard, known as Coeur de Lion, the Lion-Hearted, was indeed a prisoner when the poem was written. He had been crowned king of England before leaving that country in 1190, to join the Third Crusade. His prowess and his exploits on that long bloodbath were recounted all across Europe and quickly became legendary. He had ardent followers, but he had made enemies not only among the Saracens but among the European heads of state in the coalition that had assembled at the pope's bidding. There was a popular belief in England that Richard, who barely spoke English, would never return from the Crusade to see his own new kingdom.

In 1192 he fell sick with a fever that weakened him all through that summer, and he had not recovered when, one October night, as secretly as possible, he set sail in an unescorted galley, from the port of Acre, bound for Europe. He had been warned that enemies of his among the powers of Europe were determined to prevent him from reaching his own land again. He had appealed to the Knights Templar and they had supplied him with a small band of armed men to sail with him. A chronicler by the name of Bernard le Tresorier wrote that in spite of all the care they took, one among them was sailing with them in order to betray the king.

The rest of Richard's household and family were already on their way, aboard another vessel. Their departure had not been secret and they had followed the main sea-lanes, and in time reached Sicily and Rome. Richard's galley avoided the regular routes and slipped among the islands through the less-known channels, the haunts of Greek and Barbary pirates, in order to avoid ambush. They reached Cyprus and Corfu, and from there they set out for Marseilles on the winter sea. Six weeks later, they put in at a harbor in northern Italy where Richard had friends he trusted, and there he learned that Raymond of Toulouse, angered by autocratic actions of Richard's on the eastern journey to Jerusalem, two years before, had forces lying in wait for their galley in every port from Italy to the west.

Though the seas were wild, Richard turned back to Corfu, planning to cross Europe secretly from some point farther east. Near Corfu they were approached by two Roumanian pirate ships, one of which Richard chartered. He and his immediate entourage transferred to the pirate vessel, and the ships then sailed together up the eastern Adriatic to Istria, where the winter seas grew more violent than ever and the vessel on which Richard was sailing was shipwrecked. He and others of his band were cast ashore in a region that was part of the domain of Count Leopold of Austria.

On his way back from Acre, Richard had bought three rubies from a merchant of Pisa. One of them, set in a gold ring, he had worn on the voyage. He sent a messenger, with the ring as a gift, to Count Mainerd, Leopold's vassal, whose castle commanded the coast there, and with it a request for safe conduct, under the Truce of God, for shipwrecked travelers. When the messenger was asked where these travelers were coming from he said they were returning from the Holy Land. And who were they, the count asked. One was Baldwin of Béthune, the messenger answered, and the one who had sent the ring was a merchant named Hugo.

The count turned the ring over in his hand and looked at it carefully for a long time. Finally he said, "His name is not Hugo. It is King Richard. I have sworn to arrest every pilgrim coming from there, and to accept nothing from them. But such is the value of this, and the eminence of the person who has honored me by sending it, that I return it to him, and with it the freedom to pass through this domain."

When the messenger reported this to Richard and those who were with him, they were alarmed. They managed to acquire horses, and they set out at night to cross the lands of Count Mainerd. The count, in the meantime, sent word to his brother, Frederick, through whose land the king and his party would have to pass. Frederick sent one of his most trusted men, a Norman named Roger, to search all the places in the area where pilgrims stopped for shelter, and to trace the king, if possible, by asking about any strangers who had been seen there. If Roger could find the king, Frederick promised him half of the town in which they caught him. And Roger kept asking questions until he found Richard in one of the hostelries.

At first Richard denied that he was the king, but at last he announced who he was, and invoked the Truce of God, and Roger's mercy. At that point Roger's Norman tie to Richard the Plantagenet heir proved more important to him than what his Austrian lord had charged him to do, and instead of taking Richard prisoner he burst into tears of distress at the king's situation, gave him a fine horse, and urged him to escape. Roger went back to Frederick and told him that the travelers they had suspected were Baldwin of Béthune and his friends. Baldwin was taken into custody and he allowed Frederick's men to believe that he was the king, while Richard and a small band of knights slipped away.

They traveled an incredible distance, covering the two hundred miles from the coast to the Danube near Vienna in three days and nights, although the king was still suffering from the fever that had sapped his strength for months. He and his men took lodgings in a low tavern, exhausted. A boy from their party who knew German went out to get food for them. The only money he had to pay for it was Syrian gold besants, which aroused suspicion, as the boy could see, but the king did not have the strength to set out again, and a few days later, when the boy went out he was arrested and tortured until he confessed who Richard was.

The tavern was surrounded, and when Richard saw that he was trapped he ducked into the kitchen, pulled on a scullion's smock, and started to turn the spit in the fireplace. But some of Leopold's men had been at Acre, and they recognized the king even in that disguise. Richard, when approached, said he would give himself up only to Count Leopold himself, and Leopold is said to have lost no time in going to the tavern to take prisoner the King of England, which he did with all due ceremony. Richard was taken to the castle and kept under heavy guard.

In western Europe, Richard's mother, Queen Aliénor (or, as she is generally known now, Eleanor) of Aquitaine, knew that Philip Augustus, the king of the Franks, was mustering his armies to move against her, and that in Richard's absence his younger brother, John, had made plans to join forces with Philip Augustus, who was to reward him by making him Duke of Normandy. Leopold's capture of Richard and the ominous activities in England and on the borders of Normandy were taking place at the time of the preparations for Christmas all across Europe. Three days after Christmas, Philip Augustus, in Paris, received a letter from the Holy Roman Emperor informing him that Richard was Count Leopold's prisoner. The news soon reached the English court, but nobody knew where Richard was being kept. Dignitaries from the English church—bishops, abbots, chancellors—set out in midwinter to cross southern Germany and Austria, following rumors, trying to find out where the king was.

At this point in the account of one of the chroniclers, the minstrel of Reims, the story seems to move into pure legend. Whatever the minstrel's sources may have been, he told of Richard's jongleur, or singer, Blondel, searching through Austria for his king, and taking lodgings at the foot of the rock below the tower of Durrenstein, and there hearing Richard singing one of his poems, a *tenso:* a poem written as an exchange of alternate voices. When the first stanza ended, Blondel sang the second in reply, and so they went on to the end of the poem, each certain by then of who the other was, and Blondel spread the news.

So the English knew where Richard was, but during the winter he was moved under heavy guard from castle to castle, and Count Leopold and Henry of Hohenstaufen, the Holy Roman Emperor, took their time in working out the terms and price they would set for Richard's ransom. Both of them had scores to settle with him, dating back to before the Crusade.

But whatever his relations with them may have become, in the eyes of most of Christendom Richard remained the hero of the Crusade, a figure of more than human eminence, and though the count and the emperor may have considered having him executed publicly or secretly, it was clear that they would gain little from that except enmity. It would in fact be extremely wasteful, if England and his mother wanted Richard back as dearly as apparently they did. They worked out a ransom for the king that was meant to cripple Richard's kingdom before he was returned to it. A hundred thousand marks of silver. Two hundred hostages to be chosen from the leading families of England and Normandy. The Emperor of Cyprus to be freed from the silver chains in which Richard had left him, and Aliénor of Brittany to be given in marriage to Count Leopold's son.

While the negotiations were proceeding Richard was allowed greater freedom. He took part in the Easter court functions of the Holy Roman Empire, at Speyer. The winter rest evidently had restored his health and spirits. In the course of the Easter assembly a tribunal of knights and priests was assembled to hold a kind of trial of Richard, a session whose purpose was to readjust changes that Richard had made in the intricate power structure of Europe, and to take him to task for his offenses against Leopold of Austria, the house of Montferrat, and the king of the Franks. Richard is said to have defended himself with a grace and candor that won the admiration of many of his adversaries, and made the proceedings themselves seem crude and mean exercises in vindictive persecution. In the end, when Richard knelt courteously before the emperor, in the manner of his mother's courts of chivalry at Poitiers, the emperor himself was moved to tears, raised him to his feet and seated him on the dais beside him. For a week he was the emperor's guest. Then abruptly he was imprisoned again, this time in the mountains on the borders of Swabia, in the massive castle of Trifels.

This sudden change came about because Philip Augustus, a man of restless malevolence, and morally well suited for partnership with Richard's younger brother John, had just had his invasion of Normandy blocked at Rouen, and then had learned of Richard's ransom and proposed release. He demanded an ally's share in whatever was gained from Richard's captivity, and he made it clear that he would see to it that such division of spoils was worth the emperor's cooperation.

For his part, Henry set about trying to use Philip Augustus's influence with the church in France to his own advantage, by means of a series of unsavory manipulations, and a string of murders in high places. The agreement for Richard's ransom and release had been signed and was on its way back to England, but Philip Augustus's demands led Henry to consider the possibility of reopening the bidding between the Plantagenets and the king of the Franks in some way that would direct more money into his own hands. He kept Richard under close guard while he thought over the best possible use of him as a source of profit. He was reluctant to let go of so rich a prize while there remained any chance of making something more by holding onto him. But in the course of the spring he moved Richard from Trifels to the royal court at Hagenau and allowed him the privileges of a carefully watched royal guest. And there, that spring, he and Richard came to talk of their mutual interest in poetry.

It had been a bright strand in Richard's life for as long as he could remember. His mother, Aliénor, was the granddaughter of Guilhem IX, Comte de Peitau (Count of Poitiers), who in his day was probably the most powerful ruler in Europe; his domains, at any rate, dwarfed those of the kings of France and England. In the books Guilhem is regularly referred to as the first of the troubadours, which may not have been altogether true, for it seems likely that there was a nascent lyric tradition between Poitiers and the Pyrénées before he composed his own songs. But he is the first of the troubadours whose songs— eleven of them, at least—have survived, and the originality apparent in his surviving poems suggests that he must have been an initial and compelling force in the great current of poetry, music, and conduct that came after him.

Eble II of Ventadorn, a vassal of Guilhem's, and a friend and rival of his, was also a troubadour, known as the Singer. In his court at Ventadorn, troubadours and minstrels were welcomed and encouraged—the "school of Eble" is mentioned in one of Bernart's poems—but none of his own poems survived into the age of printing.

Guilhem died in 1126. Eleven years later his heir, Guilhem X, died suddenly at thirty-eight, in questionable circumstances, and his daughter Aliénor became his heir. She was barely fifteen, but she was married to Louis, King of France (Louis VII), who was little more than a year older than she was. The marriage did not last, but they went together on the Second Crusade (1147-1149). Aliénor's discontent with the gloomy piety of Louis's cold court intensified, and the French were disappointed when she failed to produce a male heir. She and Louis were legally separated, and the marriage annulled, in 1152. She retired to her own court in Poitiers, which she was to make into the model of the chivalric courts of love, music, and poetry. Her own native language was the langue d'oc, the language of the troubadours, which her troubadour grandfather had simply called *roman*.

She had been divorced for less than two months when she married Henry Plantagenet, the Duke of Normandy, who would become Henry II of England, and Richard's father. While Aliénor was in the Limousin with Henry, Bernart de Ventadorn is generally believed to have become one of her entourage, and to have followed her from the southwest of France to Normandy, and to her court as the duchess there. She is thought to be the distant love—or one of them—to whom many of his poems are addressed. It seems probable that he followed her from Normandy to England, where Richard was born to grow up speaking Norman French and langue d'oc, or Occitan, more happily than English. From his childhood on, he knew the lore, the gossip and legends, the lives, music, and poems of the troubadours—Bernart's, perhaps, above all. They were part of his upbringing, a heritage of his mother's free-spirited, lavishly talented southern origin.

By the end of the Third Crusade, and the spring of Richard's captivity in Hagenau, the songs and manners, the conventions and the romance (since that is where the word, in most of its present sense, comes from) of the troubadours had spread from the Limousin in widening rings across all of Europe, for well over a century. They had been echoed and adapted not only in French, the language of the north (the langue d'oïl, in which the word for "yes" was "oïl" or "oui," instead of "oc," as in the south), but in the Teutonic languages, in which the forms and stanzaic schemes of the troubadour tradition were taken up by minnesingers and were soon familiar everywhere in the Germanic kingdoms. Henry of Hohenstaufen would probably have known the heritage of the troubadours best in their later, Teutonic variations, though quite possibly he could also read and write French and Occitan, and he would certainly have heard the songs of the troubadours sung in their original language. When he and Richard talked about poetry it is likely that they spoke in French. They agreed that it would be pleasant to exchange poems. Richard already had a reputation as a poet, and apparently Henry too included among his cultivated accomplishments the writing of poetry. What was suggested must have been a simple, courteous trading of verses, with no more assumption of intimacy than a game of chess.

These were—or are thought to have been—the circumstances in which Richard wrote the poem most often associated with him, the one by which he is remembered as a poet. The notes in the *Chrestomathie de l'Ancien Français* that we used as a textbook in the graduate Old French course gave textual sources but no historical or biographical information, and when I began my effort to suggest in English the force of the original words, as I imagined I heard some remnant of it across the distance of time and language, I had only the barest program-note acquaintance with the poem's origin.

When I learned more of it, years later, it was like seeing a whole landscape light up around a figure that, until then, had been a dark silhouette.

It might be as well to sort out, before going any further, some of the confusion that has accrued around the names for the language of the troubadours. Guilhem de Peitau, who is regularly spoken of as the first of them, referred to common parlance of any kind as *lati*. His own native speech was Poitevin, a dialect both geographically and linguistically situated somewhere between the langue d'oc and the langue d'oïl. He called the tongue that was current from the Pyrénées to Lombardy roman, and he wrote his poems in it, using it as a *koiné,* or shared, common language, a fact that raises the question of whether or not there may have been earlier lyric and poetic uses of it that would have been familiar to him when he set out to write. In the eastern part of the south the language was called Proensal, the tongue of Proensa, or Provence; and in the west Limozi, or the tongue of the Limousin. In official Latin it was called *lingua occitana,* a derivation from *lingua aquitana,* the tongue of Aquitaine. The names for the language and for the geographical areas were inevitably intertwined from the beginning, which is why referring to the language of the first troubadours, who came from the west, as Provençal is misleading. The poet Frédéric Mistral (1830-1914), who did come from Provence and led the great Provençal revival at the end of the nineteenth century, preferred to speak of the language as a whole, with all its local variations, as Occitan, which has become the preferred term. Following that, the language of the troubadours is Old Occitan.

Whatever Richard's reason may have been for writing his own poem in French, it exemplified the troubadour poetry of his generation, the tradition set in motion by his great-grandfather, more thoroughly than I could have known when I began to attend to it word by word. Only the lyrical vigor of the lines themselves reached me, through the baffles of partial comprehension. The music for the poem has survived, as well as the text, but though I listened to a recording of it I hardly felt closer to the original, at the time. I had not begun to learn how to listen to it. But the result of my persistence was the first translation I made that I kept (I was then nineteen), and the first translation of mine that was published, along with a few poems of my own.

‑‑‑‑‑‑‑‑‑‑

When I read it now I am chiefly aware of how different it is from what I might have done later, if I had tried it again, or from what I might perhaps make of it now. The difference becomes a measure of distance, and I am tempted to believe that I was older then, stuffier and stiffer, and have been growing younger somehow in the time between. That early translation begins, "Never man caught could muster fit excuse" (*Ja nus hons pris ne dira sa reson*). I must have felt that the laden embroidery of the English conveyed the tapestry texture of the original, but through the latter a clear song carries, even in words that had not been spoken for so long. The high sarcasm of Pound's versions of Bertran de Born and Bishop's ornate flourishes were closer to my ear at the time than Richard's own ringing irony. Now I would want a simpler formality in which the mannerisms did not get in the way of the theme and urgency of the poem. It might go like this:

No prisoner ever said what he was thinking
straight out like someone who suffers nothing
but to ease his mind he can make a song.
My friends are many but are poor at giving.
It is their shame that, with no ransom coming,
these two winters I am held.

They know it well, my barons and my men,
English, Norman, Gascon and Poitevin:

I never had so poor a companion
that I left him, to save money, in prison.
I say it not to reproach anyone,
but I am still held.

Now I can tell why dead men, as they say,
and prisoners, have no friends or family
since for silver and gold they abandon me.
It hurts me, but hurts my kin still more deeply,
for at my death they will be blamed severely
that I am so long held.

No wonder my heart is sore within me
when my own kin ravages my country.
If he had in mind the promise that we
swore, both of us, to keep mutually
I am certain that I would not long be
here confined and held.

They know full well in Anjou and Touraine,
who at this moment are rich, hale young men,
that I am far, and by strange hands held down.
They love me, but not with one gold grain.
Their splendid arms are missing on the plain
when I have long been held.

Some I have loved and love, comrades of mine,
from Caen some, and some from Percherain,
they tell me, song, cannot be counted on

though my heart toward them never was false or vain.
If they attack me now what a base thing will be done
when I am held.

Countess, sister, may your own sovereign virtue
save you and keep the one this plea is sent to
and by whom I am held.

I say none of this to the heir of Chartrain, who
is Louis' mother.

It was spring, too, around the neo-Norman tower, when I worked, years ago, on the earlier version of that poem. I had a job for the following summer in France, as a tutor, and I was getting ready to go to Europe—the place itself, not merely the story of it—for the first time. The final months at the university seemed to be full of the Middle Ages. Robert Briffault's *The Troubadours* had just been published, and I remember the excitement, shared with a few other students, at discovering A. R. Nykl's recently available *Hispano-Arabic Poetry* with its revelation of the Arabic roots of some of the central forms, themes, and attitudes of troubadour poetry, as that tradition was first coming into being. My grasp of the chronology of the period remained murky and jumbled, a long tangle of feuds in a big rambling family, the accounts of them fragmentary and unreliable. My battered and much bescribbled copy of Hill and Bergin's *Anthology of the Provençal Troubadours* included medieval biographies, or vidas, of the poets in the collection, but they were not dated. I was not a scholar, the Boutière and Schutz edition of the vidas was not yet available, and it was easy to suppose that the poems and the biographical notes about the poets were of roughly the same vintage and accuracy. It would be years before I would realize how far those "lives" often were, in time, circumstance, and veracity, from the poets they claimed to represent, and how difficult it might be to catch a glimpse of the real Bernart de Ventadorn, for example, through the fiction that had been made up for him long ago.

CHAPTER TWO

Then it might be said that years in Europe intervened. I did not use libraries there as I had at the university, and my tie to the high Middle Ages and to the troubadours continued to revolve around my reading of their great heir, Dante.

One summer in my twenties, exploring in a very old car what was then considered to be a remote part of the Quercy, in southwest France, I followed a potholed dirt road along a ridge overlooking, to the north, the Dordogne, that beautiful river which I knew even then was the one that Hölderlin had come to on his fatal, mad meander across the Auvergne. Cars were few then, and tractors seldom seen at all in the small fields bounded by old walls. Hay carts drawn by cows yoked and leaning together—not oxen, but the long-horned earth-red Salers cows that would be led back to the barns to be milked in the evening—moved slowly in the lanes, filling them from side to side. Along the ridge I came to a hamlet surrounded by shaggy fields, orchards, bits of wooded pasture, and I turned off into the long grass beside a wall. I saw the roofs of farms apparently long unused, complete with stone houses and barns, in the massive, elegant rural architecture of the Quercy, which had scarcely changed between the last of the Crusades and the First World War. But it was a living village with its own unseen day-life going on, meals at noon in kitchens, smell of oak burning in stoves, hens scratching under walnut trees, sheep in the hillside pastures. The whole of it perhaps quite aware of strangers but seeming to pay no attention as I wandered through it.

When I returned to the end of the village, I was attracted, as I had been at first, by one empty farmhouse half-buried in brambles. Its situation caught me: The way it was settled under the crest of the ridge, looking out across the wide valley from below the road, where a smaller lane led down the slope beside it at an angle. It seemed rooted in self-possession, in something that it was content to keep to itself even if it fell to ruin there. I had encountered examples of that already, and would again, in many of the old empty houses of the region whose lives, from the outside, appeared to be over.

The thicket of brambles had grown over the path to the front door, which faced south toward the road, and had made its way up onto the roof, into the tiles. To the left of the parched front door buried in its thorny tangle, another, older doorway, like a barn entrance, had been bricked up, leaving a single opening the size of half a brick. I peered though the hole into the half-dark of an empty, ruined room. As my eyes adjusted to the shadow in there I saw cupped floorboards with gaping holes in them, piles of rubble and bird droppings, light from another opening, through a stone arch on the far side of the house. I had come upon an enclosed silence and a smell of stone that is still there. When I turned back to the afternoon an old man was watching me from the road.

Faded beret, shining on top in a ring from leaning into the flanks of cows, on the milking stool. Gaulish moustache, black jacket dimmed to gray, sash like a bandage, a slight stoop of the shoulders, an impression of smiling but reserved authority, and of unhurried vigor and strength. He asked whether I was looking for something. I said I was admiring the house. "Ah," he said, and nodded. I said I thought it was beautiful. "It's old," he said. I said it appeared to have been empty for a long time. "Yes," he said, "that is true. It's been empty for a long time." "It's a beautiful village," I said. "Well—," he said, and looked away. I said I hoped it had been all right to leave the car there in the long grass, but I had seen no one to ask. "Imagine," he said. "It's not in anyone's way." All at once he was being the host. I could see that he was torn between curiosity and a schooled inhibition about asking questions, but that he was determined to be the authority, in the village, on foreign visitors. "Your car license is English," he said. "You are English." The question sounded like a statement. I told him that I lived in England but was an American. "That's very far away," he said. I looked across the river. The ridges to the north, beyond the valley, looked to me like ranges of hazy hills, one behind the other, in summer along the Allegheny in western Pennsylvania, the sight of which had held me still with a sudden longing, as though they were something I recognized, when I was a child.

In the following days, continuing to explore, sometimes with the guidance of new friends met by chance in the neighborhood, I came back more than once to that same village and the uninhabited house half-hidden in brambles. My vocation as a tourist has always been dubious. Reading a guidebook and then glancing up to identify what the résumé has been summarizing is likely to seem to me, quite soon, like an exercise in alienation. I am more given to imagining what it might be like to spend time in a given spot, to get to know the sounds and the light, the people and the faces of the buildings, and how some of it had come to look the way it did. Empty houses invite the notion of living in them, looking out of their windows, being embraced and known by them. Possessing and being possessed by them. It is childish make-believe, and I played it day after day, in that countryside with its apparently inexhaustible wealth of houses that had been occupied for years only by bats, swallows, and dormice.

There were castles and *manoirs* of all sizes, some of them reduced to being used as barns, with their towers crumbling, and portals cemented over. It was a continuing treasure hunt, finding them, trying to learn something of their current status, imagining life in them at one stage or another of their past, picking up shards of latter-day gossip, which often seemed to be all that was left of their history. But I could scarcely imagine having one of them and living in it—not even in one of those dilapidated structures that had fallen on hard times, and were the ones that appealed to me most. They were too big, not only in their physical dimensions and demands but in the impositions, the assumptions built into them, the roles they embodied as long as they remained standing. I imagined that having one of them and living in it would mean being taken over by, and incorporated into that grandiose masonry. I could entertain no such fancy, even if I had had the money to acquire such a noble wreck, and I had none. Or what almost anyone else would have considered to be nothing at all. Which made the make-believe apparently quite safe.

There were mills, their deep, hunched walls and arches often as massive and splendid as the stonework of the castles. Most of them were built in settings of entrancing beauty, in woods along small rivers, or in cloven embrasures of overhanging cliffs at the bends of sinuous valleys. From almost every window there was the sight of water—ponds and races, falls and receding rapids— and all through the millhouses the sound of water came rustling, roaring, trickling, whispering, splashing, and with it the smells of water mint and wet stone, and of ancient wood that never dried. The heavy elegance and the histories of all those monuments to purpose were arched over water, which was inseparable from their lives and from their seductive nature. They were never silent. The water flowing past and through them turned them into instruments, each giving out a continuous chord, a bass note under every conversation, every word spoken there, under footsteps and the opening and closing of doors. The chord itself was hypnotic, the unceasing voice of a muffled creature held behind the walls. In a lower room of some of the mills, a trapdoor in the heavy boards of the floor could be levered up like a drawbridge, and the moment it began to open a hollow roar burst from under it like a genie, the thunderous echo of a waterfall in a cavern, and the whole building stood astride that deafening shout day and night, summer and winter. I was hearing it in the summer, when the sunlight reached down earliest into those clefts in the valleys and stayed in them longest, but I could tell by looking up at the cliffs how short and dark the winter days must be, with the presence of water in everything, never warm, never reduced, the sheets never dry on the beds, nor anything else, and the magnificent mills did not strike me as good places to spend the winter.

Though there was one, not set in a gorge but in the basin of a valley, beside a small stream, with the millrace running not under but along one side of it, the south side, so that the surface of the water and the walls rising above it caught the sun most of the day. The long, graceful building was made of red sandstone, with a series of windows overlooking the stream, and a spacious room at the lower end looking down the valley under lime trees. On the far side of the stream, the top of the railroad embankment, where the tracks ran for a short distance between tunnels, was visible here and there through the treetops. In later years I would watch closely, as the train I was on emerged from the tunnel, and try to catch a glimpse of the red sandstone mill, down by its stream, before the darkness swept it away again.

The man who took me there the first time, with the keys and the airs that went with them, was the gatekeeper at the railroad crossing a few miles along the line, a large man with a wheeze and a ponderous middle, a swollen nose, a black peaked cap, and an ear attuned to anything that might be turned to his advantage. The mill, he said, had not been used for its original purpose for a long time, and the rest of the house had long been above such activities. It belonged to two sisters living in town, both of them very old, who spoke to almost nobody, but he said he had their confidence, and he made that sound exclusive. It had been years since the sisters had lived in the house at all, and some time now since they had even been out to see it. The roof needed repair. There were places where the building had begun to be unsafe, but he had no wish to dwell upon such aspects of it. There were piles of ancient furniture stacked under bed sheets, with the leaks from the ceiling rotting them. Again and again, passing between the tunnels, I wondered whatever had become of the sisters and of him, as year by year the top of the mill sank through the trees.

Some of the closed farmhouses held a more plausible attraction. They seldom stood all by themselves. Even when the farms were sited on hillsides, facing across slopes toward far ridges, the stone houses almost always had stone barns beside them—or even built inside the same walls under the same roof—and other stone buildings forming a barnyard or courtyard, partly enclosed, with walls completing the circuit. The distinct rural architecture, with outside stone stairs, roofed porches, huge stone fireplaces, stone arches in which the dishes were—or had been—washed and drained, and the barns, henhouses, pig sheds, cisterns, well houses, all in stone, were built to an ancient vision of all such things, in accord with conventions and proportions many of which had been taken for granted before the fourteenth century. Some of the walls along the lanes were said to date from the time of the Romans, who had made—or had forced the inhabitants to make—cobbled lanes for the tramp of the legions. The stone-and-timber structure of the dry walls of barns repeated that of some of the fortifications built in the days of Caesar, or so it was said in the cool of dark cow byres, where the cows stood chewing in the middle of the summer day. The stone roofs of the oldest buildings were descendants of the stone roofs of the Gauls, and the roofs of outdoor stone ovens and of shepherds' shelters overlooking wooded slopes and pastures were constructed of huge slabs of limestone layered and shaped into domes, like beehives, replicas of originals more ancient than the Romans. On most buildings the stone roofs had given way, gradually, to thatch, more steeply pitched, on wooden beams and rafters, and the thatch in turn had been replaced by flat red tiles. Often the barns were set on slopes, with two floors. The upper one was entered from the upper slope, through doors set in a high arch, and the lower level was half set into the ground, and was entered from down on the slope, through a door on the side. The high, tented roofs swept down in a graceful curve, almost to the ground, on the upper level, flaring out into rows of flat stones along the eaves, in a shape like the upturned wings of sailing hawks. Even those farms that were set farther apart than most were seldom more than a few minutes' walk from a small hamlet, a cluster of farmhouses gathered back to back, each facing out toward its home fields and kitchen gardens. The solidity, the proportions, the openness to the sun and daylight, the prospects of rolling hills and far ridges, made it possible for me to imagine waking under one of those roofs, looking out through plum and walnut branches in one season or another, hearing the village sounds of animals and humans as I heard them in the course of those summer days, and the sounds of the woods near the houses on the uplands.

Those buildings in which lives had begun and ended appealed to a lingering fancy that I had supposed might never be more than that, of somehow having—or at least knowing—a quiet rural place close to the world around me and a long step away from the assumptions of the metropolitan circumstances in which I spent most of my life and from which my mind was seldom altogether removed, any more than I would ever be separated from my native language. Such a place would foster a sense of distance both in geography and in time, a secrecy of its own. The fantasy, I knew, welled up out of childhood, from sources some of which were subject to no recall. But there were two of them that I had never forgotten.

Both came from when I was nine or so. My family moved then from Union City, New Jersey, where my father's yellow brick church—demolished soon after we left—stood on the Palisades above Hoboken Harbor and the Hudson. A huge van that seemed as big as the house and filled the whole width of Fourth Street, breaking branches on the old poplar trees, was parked in front of the house for most of a day while every object that had figured in our lives was loaded into it, or so it seemed until I realized that some things were going to be left behind. Those would include the easel that a member of the congregation had made and given to me because I was going to be a painter. It was left standing out on the grass by the fence.

The van had a big globe on the side, and a scroll saying "The World Moves. So Does Post"—something that my father thought I should find admirable. And then it was gone, and we drove, four of us, in the high blue Buick the same age that I was, to the coal mining city of Scranton, Pennsylvania, deep in hard times and trying to believe it had not always been like that.

The first summer there, through the good offices of a family in the church, my father rented us a lakeside cottage, somewhat neglected, with a leaky roof, in the woods beyond Elk Mountain. I say that my father had rented it for us—my mother, my sister and me—because only he had use of the car. He spent most of the week in town, leaving the three of us up at the lake. There was a counter-front general store along the back road on the far side of the lake, and the Arrowhead van came by every few days with groceries, but although my mother loved being there she chafed at not being able to go anywhere except in the rowboat, to friends across the lake, until my father drove up from town, usually on a Saturday, and always unannounced. No one had a telephone. To me the run-down cottage, and the lake and the woods, and the way we lived there, were a joy beyond anything I had known was possible.

And not having my father there was like having the sky clear after weeks of rain. A few years later when he left for Europe as an army chaplain during the war, and I went away to school and college, and he had not been part of my days for a long time, I tried in a fumbling way to make an idol of him, without a clear understanding of what I was doing. The effort was encouraged in part by my own isolation and by finding myself repeatedly in situations where I knew no one. I had no other male elder in the back of my mind, to refer to. In order to keep the image of my father that I wanted, I had to annul the memory of his unvarying remoteness, his restrictions, which had no parallels in the families of my schoolmates, his unpredictable severity throughout the years of my childhood.

But I was still at an age when it is possible to live day and night in some condition of existence, and even look back through it, without ever assigning a name to it, an identifying caption that might help one to step outside it. There had been no word for that remoteness before he went away. It was the way the world was, and it partook of, and was a proof of his unremitting, unquestioned pastoral duties, since he was a Presbyterian minister with a role around him that included the whole family as the supporting cast. His position, as he thought of it, and the injunctions that emanated from it, through him, prevented me from having much to do with other children except in the classroom and Sunday school, and the moody caprice with which his commandments were enforced suggested a growing wish for me not to be there at all.

In the Scranton years his anxieties increased and he and my mother reached an impasse, but it seemed that the poles of their magnets had been reversed some years before that.

At the lake, the list of what was forbidden was longer than ever. It included regulating how far I might go from the cottage, forbidding ever getting into a boat alone, ever carrying a knife, striking a match, or climbing a tree. But he was not there, and my mother's rule was for us not to let him catch us doing any of the things he had outlawed, and not to get hurt doing those things.

The cottage we had, that first year, was set back from the lake, in the woods, and the woods were freedom. Old beeches overhanging the water, red birch and white birch, hickory, oaks, and conifers—I came to know the trees as individual members of another family. There were a few other children in the lakeshore cottages, and some of us built a platform in the beech limbs.

Not far behind the cottage, in the woods along a slope, was a small clearing with thorn and blackberry and laurel bushes deep around it. A tunnel under the laurels led into another, smaller clearing where suddenly everything appeared to be different. Light came through the green of all the leaves and the grass. The sounds were furred, as though they were coming across water, or echoed around a corner, or remembered. The circle of sky overhead, with the ends of branches playing its edges, looked complete, not merely part of the sky outside, where I had come from. The first time I found myself there I sat on the grass and moss and looked around me with a rising flush of amazement and tenderness, as though I knew the place. My heart pounded. At one end of the enclosure the moss was deep and I lay down, looking up through the leaves, wanting to stay there.

But I did not want to be called while I was there. I did not want my name to come to me there from anywhere else, and I did not want to call out to somewhere else from there. So I never dared stay as long as I would have liked to, and I never let myself fall asleep there, though I thought how I would like to wake up and find I was there. I never even closed my eyes there for long. Yet I was still enough for many birds to come to the bushes, and for snakes to emerge and stop like films, sunning themselves. They were some of the first wild creatures I had ever seen. When I left I tried to brush the grass upright again, to leave no sign of my having been there. I did not feel that I had been hiding, but that something about the place itself was secret and fragile and must not be betrayed, a presence like the nearness of a bird. I went there often that summer, sometimes staying only long enough to make sure that it was really there. I never quite expected to find it again.

The other source came from before we actually moved to Scranton, when we were planning to move there. I remember the note of good news being discussed, as the two women talked quietly in the farmhouse dining room. One of them was my mother and the other was a woman a year or two older, thin, fine, her hair already turning white. They had met in a park in Union City, to which they took their children. The other woman, whose name was Esther, had two sons just older than I was.

There was a sadness about Esther that made my mother sigh and look away when she spoke of her. They became close friends who lowered their voices when they talked to each other. Esther had taught school before she had the boys, and her education was an element in the sympathy between them. Almost as soon as they met, my mother knew that Esther would soon be leaving. A marriage breaking up, whether because of hopeless disaffection, abuses of some kind, or another person, was never clear to me. My mother would not speak of it, but I could see its darkness around the few words she ventured about Esther's unjust lot, before the subject was put firmly away. The very idea of divorce was inadmissible to my father, even though one couple—the man a minister and a seminary classmate of my father's, and both of them friends of my parents in their first years together—had divorced and were still spoken of with an indulgent fondness colored by their feeling for that time which had ended for all of them.

Esther's parents had a farm in northeastern Pennsylvania, where she and the boys had been spending more and more time, and before long she moved there with them. They all helped her parents in the house and on the farm. We went up there to visit them a few times and were welcomed as part of the family. By the time we first saw the farm the boys talked and behaved as though they had never lived anywhere else.

Esther's father was a tall, round man, gentle and quiet, who did most of the farm work himself and was often down at the barn or out in a field. Her mother had a face like an apple, the mouth and eyes no more than deep creases in a perpetual smile. The rest of her was a series of spheres, like a snowman's, in a faded flowered dress and gray apron. I do not remember her ever saying more than a few consecutive syllables as she revolved slowly in the kitchen with its gray-painted floor, and through the outer storerooms and laundry room and woodshed and cellar and dairy room. Esther's father smelled of the barn and the dairy, and her mother smelled of the stove and the laundry and of water, and neither smell was particularly fresh or good in itself, but I cherished them both possessively as though they were living things that I was allowed to claim as friends.

Their farmhouse was a white frame building set with its back to a cut near the top of a long hill, with several big maples between it and the back road to Madisonville. A long porch ran along the house on the side toward the road, under the trees. A porch with no railing, only two steps up from the ground, and it continued around the corner and all the way across the long side of the house that faced down the slope toward the valley. The drive from the road led in behind the trees and the house, and past the outbuildings, to the older barn where the sheep lived, and on down the hill to the cow barn with its silo at the far end.

When I think of it now I realize that the house must have been built in the early years of the twentieth century, perhaps on the site of an earlier house, but I did not imagine time and age in that way then. I took it for granted that the farm and the house had been there, just as they were, forever, and that Esther's father and mother, and their parents—I had met her grandfather the first time I went there—had known the place all their lives.

I can see now that it must have been a poor, expiring farm, already well into its last years, with its one big, old white horse, its half dozen cows and a bull, twenty or thirty sheep and a dozen pigs, rusting harrow and hay rake, all in the keeping of one wheezing, overweight, white-haired man, his amiable face a network of red veins—and by two eager boys trying to talk as though their voices had broken. But the farm at once became, and would remain for me, the model of all farms. Even on the first visits there my father's attendance kept to a pattern that had become familiar. He would drive us there, perhaps stay for a cup of coffee in the parlor with the big chairs, the samplers on the walls, the side table with the huge family Bible, and he would talk to them about the affairs of his church. Then he would have things to do, people he must see, and he would drive off and come back for dinner or supper, or come back sometime later to fetch us. And while he was gone I would be allowed to go out with the boys, safe on their home ground, in their superior age. They showed me where the weasel came from, and how you lead a cow in, how to climb inside a silo, how to avoid a hayfork, and get a horse to follow you, and watch a bull, and feed pigs.

A few times we stayed there for several days. There were enough rooms for each of us to have our own, and I lay hearing the maple leaves brush the house and the windows at night, and tried to believe I was where I was. One day, for some reason that I do not remember, I was alone in the house with my mother and Esther. They were sitting at the dining room table, in the afternoon, with the dark blue water glasses set out in their places around the empty table, and were talking in low voices. I said I wanted to go out for a walk and my mother said that would be all right. You know where the bull is, Esther said, and I told her I did.

Past the old barn with its ancestral tools standing motionless in their cobwebs and sunbeams, and the smell in there of moldy straw, dry wood, and sheep. Out past an unkempt apple orchard, a green field, to fields beyond it on a hillside. It was a spring day, with the sun already starting to go down. I came to the top of a rise at the end of the fields, and suddenly the world opened and unrolled before me. A broad green meadow sloped away at my feet in a long, spreading curve like the back of a wave, to deep woods at the far end, a line of trees rising all along the bright green of the grass that lay around it like an arm, where the meadow leveled out, and where it curved like a wide river, around to the right, toward the sun.

All of it glowed without a sound as I stared from the hilltop. I do not know how long I stood there held by the radiance of that silent valley. I did not step forward into it.

Then it was cold, and I turned back the way I had come. My mother asked where I had gone, and I tried to say something about the far valley I had seen, though I felt shy talking about it, as though it was a mistake to say anything, and yet I wanted to tell them how beautiful it was, and I knew as I tried to that the words conveyed nothing at all about it.

Esther said, "Oh, that's the night pasture."

The night pasture is not there to be seen again, nor the farm itself as I saw it last, one spring morning when I had been camping, with the brothers, down near the pump house and the pond, and we watched, on the far hill, a man, a mule, and a boy, climbing the furrows, planting potatoes. I went back years later and found the place where it had been. The whole of the farm below the cow barn, and the night pasture over the hill, had been pawed out, and in their stead was the empty air over a freeway.

Yet some residue of those two places remained with me and returned without being called, that summer in the Quercy, and it must have formed part of the lure of the abandoned farmhouses there, which in time would lead me back to elaborate songs in an archaic language.

An old Englishman, an unconventional—some said cranky—agronomist who had found his way to that region in the years after the Second World War, had flung himself happily and without question into the remains of the peasant agriculture of the valley, harmonizing it in his mind, no doubt, with his own childhood, and with the early hopes of the English soil movement and the vision of Sir Albert Howard and predecessors as far back as Cobbett.

He presented a convert's projection of it—insistent, partial, eccentric, a little ridiculous, yet sustained by the beauty and the apparent stability and benevolence of the life he had adopted. I listened with some skepticism to his doctrine but I admired his vegetable garden and his fruit trees and the evident peace of his days, his sense of abundance, his love of what he had come to. Doubter though I was, I welcomed glimpses that he afforded me of the farms and farming of his neighbors in the village, with whom he had worked at the haying and harvesting, and other labors that were still done in common, and I gained some notion of the ways of a farming village there that I could not have come to so quickly on my own.

On what I thought might be my last visit to the empty house on the ridge above the river, I saw the old man with whom I had spoken on the first day, and asked him whether he knew who owned the place. Yes, he said, he knew. I asked again and he told me her name and said that she had married a colonel and they had lived in the colonies, but now he was retired and they had come back and lived over in Miers, and the colonel worked as the ticket agent at the Gouffre de Padirac. I asked whether he thought she might sell it. "You want to buy it?" he asked. The idea seemed unimaginable to him. I said I was not sure but had thought of asking. "You can ask," he said.

He told me how to find her.

The *place* at Miers was patrolled by a raven. Inquiries about the raven directed me in due course to the owner of the uninhabited farmhouse, and I called on her, a peasant woman who had lived all her adult life as the wife of a provincial army officer in French West Africa, a region colored mauve on the maps of my childhood. She wanted to talk of tropical discomforts and diseases, and of worms living for years under her skin. She still had one there in her arm, and she put my finger on it. She spoke with a condescending patience of the people of the region she and her husband had come back to. She said they had never changed at all. But their quaint ways were now part of her décor: copper basins and warming pans were hanging on the walls, and a red-checked pelmet under the wooden mantel of the fireplace in her sitting room, into which the afternoon light arrived through orange-tinted windows.

I had told her at the beginning that I had seen the empty house and wanted to ask her about it. When I did, her eyes filled with tears. "That is the house I was born in," she said. She told me, as the old man had, that no one had lived in it for thirty-five years, and that it had been used for a time for drying tobacco in, which she did not like to think of.

"Now they don't even do that," she said. I asked her whether she might ever consider selling it. "Oh," she said, "I don't like to think of selling the house I was born in." She wiped her eyes with her apron. Nobody spoke. Then she drew in her breath and said, "There was a woman who wanted to buy it once and we talked about it. That was a few years ago." "What happened?" I asked. She shrugged. "Nothing," she said. "Did you consider selling it to her?" I asked. "Yes," she said. "We even agreed on a price. But then it never happened. That was before the war. She went away and I never heard from her."

"And would you think of selling it now?" I asked. "To you?" she asked. I nodded. Her husband was listening, without a word. "I wouldn't want to sell it to anyone for speculating," she said.

"The house I was born in." Another pause and then she asked, "What would you want it for?" "Not for speculation," I said. "Would you want it to live in, yourself?" she asked. I could tell that it seemed unlikely to her. "Yes," I said.

"If you wanted it to live in, I might sell it for that," she said. "How much would you want for it?" I asked. "I wouldn't ask you more than the price I agreed on with that woman," she said. I asked her how much that was, thinking that it had been frivolous, and indeed unfair to her, to pursue the matter that far, since I did not have enough money to buy anything like a house.

Years earlier, when I had been at college, a cousin of my mother's, a schoolteacher who had never married, had left me, at her·death, the sum of eight hundred dollars. It was all that remained of her savings after her funeral expenses had been paid. My mother had put the money into Treasury bonds and I had never touched it. Over the years it had grown by half. That was the sum I dangled in my mind to allow me to play the house-hunting game at all, and in fact it had led me first to the old English agronomist, who had proposed acting as an agent for a neighbor, to sell me what he called a cottage that would be within my means. But when I had gone to see it what I found was a sheep shed in a side valley, with what he described as a generous ladder to the hayloft, and a kitchen consisting of a gas burner and a basin on a bench.

But the sum the woman who had been born in the house named to me was the exact figure that my great-aunt's small inheritance amounted to at that time, and I held out my hand in agreement.

Then I had to begin to earn money to repair the roof and floors and cistern. I was twenty-six, with no money at all and a house in the depths of the country in France. In all the years that followed, the house, the remains of the farm, the village, became a constant, insistent part of my life, invaluable, cherished, demanding, inescapable. I would return there after months away in cities in other countries and be swept up again by the sight of the roofs of the village, and the great valley opening beyond them to the north and west, beyond the river. The beauty of the land and of the human presence on it kept alive and deepened an attachment that seemed rooted somewhere I could not remember. And even with my small earnings the house and garden were for years a haven, relatively self-possessed, with an apparently inexhaustible time of its own.

For several years after I bought it I spent the winters in London, scratching out a freelance existence (with no sense of its being precarious) under the auspices of a few producers of the BBC Third Programme. Then years in the farmhouse year-round, and others with the winters in New York.

CHAPTER THREE

Even before I went to the Quercy, I was aware that the region, the valley itself and the country to the north and south of it, was the land of the troubadours. The common use of the word Provençal for their language and poetry suggests, as the setting for them, the landscape of Provence, of Vence and the Vaucluse and Les Baux. In fact the original homeland of that poetry was much farther to the west. The earliest centers of the troubadour tradition that are known to us, as well as the first great courts of chivalry and courtly love, were in the southwest, in Poitiers and Toulouse.

I knew that, of course, during those first years overlooking the river, watching the seasons change there, and then living around the full cycle of them in that country. From time to time I returned to my anthology of the troubadours. But though some of the poems and *vidas* were more or less familiar by then, they remained like odd tatters of a disintegrated tapestry, single pieces surviving from a once brilliantly colored puzzle, elegant but isolated and adrift in poor light. My groping sense of the texts themselves relied upon literal translations into modern French, and glossaries and a few pages of rudimentary grammar, which were never adequate.

And yet the language—a wholly peasant and much later form of what Guilhem IX and Bernart de Ventadorn had referred to as their *lati*—was all around me.

My wife at the time I went to live there and I were the first inhabitants of the village, for as long as anyone could remember or had heard of, who were not peasants, not from the region, not French at all. Even the nuns who had lived in the village, teaching school in one house or another (the old man whom I had first met there told me that he had learned to read and write in the farmhouse I had moved into), were probably from peasant families in the region. And the language that everyone of my own age and older spoke in the village was not French but what they referred to as *patois,* a word connoting no status at all, but something relegated to a dialect or lingo.

I spoke of it, and its history, with respect and they responded politely but without belief. Their actual parlance was probably as far from the language of the troubadours as modern English is from that of Shakespeare—perhaps even that of Chaucer—but it was still Occitan, and I listened to it every day in conversations at the entrances to fields, in shops and markets and the streets in the towns, and in the lanes and on the still unpaved road outside the garden wall, until I could catch phrases, then follow subjects and sometimes a whole sentence. It was like learning by oneself to catch fish by the gills in the river. But the sound and the inflection grew familiar. I even learned to mumble a few phrases, to the amusement of my neighbors.

The children in the village when I went there grew up to be bussed away to schools in towns—a new practice. There they were discouraged both officially and socially from speaking patois, and came to regard the very knowledge of it as a stigma, a proof of being rural, hence backward and poor, and the name of progress was invoked once again in the cause of the destruction of language.

I regret that I did not pay far closer and more determined attention to the latter-day Limozi while it was still current all through the days. One neighbor, a woman of my own age, taught me words, phrases, an occasional proverb, and they came to be a kind of confidence we shared, like family jokes, along with discussions over the garden wall about tomato wilt, and transplanting leeks, and strangers seen walking in the village, and how the fire had started in the empty barn on the upland. But at that time there were no courses given in the language, no grammars or dictionaries available, no teachers that I knew of. My friend had no experience in teaching a language in any systematic way. Her days were filled with the work in the vegetable garden, the fields, the house and barnyard, and all that was required of her in bringing up three children. She would never have been able to conceive of taking the time that would have been needed, regularly, to try to teach patois to anyone. The very thought of doing that would have seemed embarrassing, incongruous, and slightly improper to her. And to me, the prospect of really learning patois never seemed quite tangible. I could not have followed my neighbors around making them self-conscious with my efforts to seize and mimic every word they uttered, and my desire to learn their disregarded language, if pressed upon them too intently, would have become wearisome and suspicious to them and to me, too. Their ancient tongue was growing hard to believe in, so that even trying to learn it seemed a little folksy.

And although from the first weeks in the region, and the early explorations of old, empty, sometimes abandoned or ruined buildings, the awareness of the deep past was inseparable from the lure of the land, which soon held me there, and the structures themselves appeared to me as palimpsests of unsounded age, I did not at once start any systematic study of the history of the area, and did not set about trying to find traces of the troubadours. Fragments of the history came my way, by chance, from hearsay, and I found books in junk stores or they were lent to me by friends. The *département* had a historical society with an erudite bulletin, and I read what turned up there, and certainly did not avoid chances to be informed about some moment or circumstance of local antiquity. I retained a distant, dim, schoolbook recollection of French history, worse lit in some places than others. But in those first years in the village I put off until some later time any concerted attempt to form a coherent, but detached, knowledge of that part of the world as it had once been. The study of that as a portable subject in print was abstract and remote compared to the past that clearly inhabited every aspect of the life around me and the objects that filled it. It was memory, in the fabric of that life and its perspectives of survival, rather than anything so withdrawn, codified, separated out as history, that drew me, like someone trying to wake me.

The village that I had first come to along the unpaved cart track was another time, set in itself, and acceding—as it rose, day by day, to the calendar of fêtes distributed annually by the postal service—to an unquestioned round. I laughed off much of the old English agronomist's fantasy of the region's idyllic farm life, yet I could see some of the things that had led him to embrace it as a creed.

From the viewpoint shared by many journalists, economic theorists, the ministry of agriculture, and go-ahead professionals in the towns, that part of France as a whole, and that département in particular, were hopelessly backward, and it was the village life, peasant agriculture, that held it mired in the bad old days. There were economic charts of France on which the area figured as one of the poorest sections of the country, but the life I saw around me in the village did not strike me as impoverished except in the limitation of its horizons. Medical care was covered by the government. The local schoolmaster was a dedicated, impassioned, widely read man with an ardent love of the region and its past, and in their first school years the children received a remarkably thorough primary education. Everyone was proud of how well they ate. "When I was a child," the roofer told me, "we didn't always have much to eat, but now every day is like a wedding." Everyone dressed comfortably, dolled up for fêtes, bundled up for the winter. Because of the decline in population during and after the great wars, most families had more buildings and more land than they really used. But time itself, the pace of the days and the leisure it allowed, was the luxury that was taken for granted and barely recognized. Many of those who became my friends lived to look back upon that pace wistfully as a thing of the past, in kitchens filled with laborsaving devices.

There were two cars in the village then, both of them old. One was the roofer's van. I could hear its motor humming like a saw blade, leaving the village in the morning, coming back in the evening, when he was working on a roof far enough away to warrant it. Otherwise, if the job was not far from the village, he would leave the car in the barn and walk. The other car, dating from the end of the First World War, was a tall green and black sedan, with braided hand ropes and flower vases inside, a bar for a lap robe, and the battery on the running board. It belonged to the leading family of the village, owners of many hectares of land and of barns and farmhouses that they left standing empty. The car, proud relic of an earlier day in the family history, was trundled out every few weeks to go to the fair or a baptism or a wedding, or to church when they had guests.

Most of the village and the neighboring hamlets still worked together on some of the farm labors, especially in the ritual care of the vineyards—hoeing, pruning, and of course the harvesting, the *vendange*. After working together in one of their orchards or fields or vineyards, they gathered in one of their houses and ate together, at midday or later in the afternoon, depending on what the work was, and how far away from the village. One way or another they found a moment after work, most days when the weather was fair, to wander along and sit for a while on the stone ledge built into the wall of the overgrown field in the middle of the village, and catch up on things with their neighbors. In Occitan. I did not realize, because of youth, I suppose, and because I did not allow myself to believe it, that I was watching the last years when things would happen like that, and that soon I would seldom mention, as though it were slightly embarrassing, how recently I had stood among men singing together as they swung mattocks in the vineyards out on the east slope below the cliff.

I knew that I had strayed into an unguarded part of the past that had managed to remain coherent and in place, leading back from season to season, life to life, farther than I could imagine. The human presence there was continuous in the ground all the way back to the caves at Pêche-Merle and the burials at La Chapelle-aux-Saints and the retreating fringes of the Ice Age. Intimations of such continuity were seductive. I had never encountered anything of the kind in my own half-known origins, for neither of my parents had relayed to me a credible awareness of the past, either their own or that of their antecedents, and we had moved from place to place where they had no memories, no prior attachments. But in the village, old tools in the barns, pairs of wheels leaning in corners, had not entirely left the lives in which they had moved and turned and shone in that very place. Local details of unknown origin were taken for granted as part of the fabric of the world. Recipes for green walnut leaf liqueurs and for ratafia, for instance. Draperies of carefully made string mesh, arranged across the faces of yoked cows as they worked, to keep the flies from their eyes. Even bits of lore that sounded like little more than superstition were surviving shards of a more vigorous and imposing order. Georges Gras telling me to tie a string around a tree before transplanting it, with the knot on the north side, so that I would have it facing the right way when I planted it in the new place, and the sun would pass over it the way the tree was used to.

I did not ascribe a prelapsarian perfection to that past which I glimpsed in fragmentary revelations from my neighbors. I was constantly reminded of the strand of meanness, the harshness, the discomfort and cold that were part of their lives, and of the unheeded sufferings of animals raised for slaughter. My own origins—my past, in fact, such as it was—flickered warnings against unwary attachment to antiquity for its own sake, and a foreign antiquity at that, haunted by a suspicion of unreality. Yet I was drawn by the remains of an existence that I could never join even if I wanted to. Its presence ran through my days there and I prized it as a great stroke of luck.

One attractive element in the farming life that had evolved by then in the Quercy was an unobtrusive independence of spirit, a quality rooted in the practice of *polyculture*—the growing of more or less everything. It was an immemorial system encouraged by the variations of the crumpled landscape with its small irregular fields fitted into the stony contours, but deplored by theorists as inefficient, an impediment to the abstraction of agriculture and the relegation of it as a way of life. Its assumptions included having extended families loosely clustered in and around the small hamlets, each family owning plots of land of several kinds scattered within walking distance of where they lived. Most families possessed a few hectares of upland woods, a few hectares of open pasture in different places, a few hectares of arable land, which they farmed on a careful four-year system of rotation, a sizable number of ritually tended walnut trees, at least one vineyard, and at least one vegetable garden, besides which they grew their potatoes, often their peas and green beans, pumpkins, squash and corn for pigs, fodder beets for pregnant ewes and for lambs, in the fields closest to home. They grew much of what they ate, and all that they fed to their animals. They sold walnuts, plums, milk, wool, calves, lambs, cheese, and they raised tobacco some years as a cash crop. They thought that was the way it had always been. In the valleys the walls were beginning to be leveled year by year to enlarge the fields for mechanization, but on the slopes and ridges and out on the lime-stone plateaus the thin soil was spread unevenly in the waves of stone, and although in the sixties the planners in the capital inaugurated programs designed to eradicate the peasantry alto-gether, the imposition of a rational grid on the uplands was hampered and delayed by the terrain.

The old ways were eroding, slipping away as I came to know them, and yet for years they lingered and were taken for grant-ed, like the faces of friends growing older. Ours was a farming village, like all the hamlets in the commune. The animals came and went in the lanes and paths, at their hours, and I knew the sounds of each family's cow bells, sheep bells, and the voices of neighbors and their dogs urging and reminding them. I learned how fragile the web had become. Most of the children left when they grew up. There were moments when the end seemed to have arrived. The year when, under the auspices of the Common Market, the sudden import of factory-raised lamb wiped out in one season all the profit in lambs raised on open pastures and fat-tened on beets grown in the fields, in the traditional way. And then the appearance of the first industrial fattening barns at the edge of one hamlet after another, and the new rotten-fish smell of them drifting through the hollows that before that had smelled of earth and oak woods. But much of the fabric survived in the generation that still spoke patois as a first language, and while it was there I was more intent on the threads of its continuity than on a determined exploration of local history that would have been unfamiliar both to me and to my neighbors who were its distant heirs.

Then I went away and was gone for twelve years.

CHAPTER FOUR

The house was occupied during my absence. And whatever changes came about in my own life, I imagined the village just as it was when I had last seen it, one winter day when a neighbor had driven me to the railroad station. Yet I had learned, through those years, of the deaths of old friends, one by one, like single strokes of a faraway bell. M. Duport, the roofer with the soft voice, who had diabetes, and suffered from sciatica even as he stood on the ladder, emerging from a roof like a figure rising from the sea, to set his tiles or hang his slates with steady deliberation. Esther who sat in the chimney corner and talked of two things only, the arthritis in her knees ("You can't know how I suffer") and animals, which she loved passionately and executed regularly—chickens, ducks, pigeons—for the kitchen. Edouard who had seen me peering into the empty house that first day, the village elder who bicycled off every Sunday afternoon to play *manille* in the café in the next village, and who remembered Verdun and never said a word about it. M. Viellescazes, the oldest of them all, who sat on the wall under the walnut tree, through the summer afternoons, in his broad black hat, his black jacket, and gray-and-black striped morning trousers, remembering stories his father had told him. The whole family of the Cavaniés, the father who had been gassed in the First World War, the bedridden mother, the sons who got drunk and bicycled a wavering line to the next village in quest of more. All of them remained part of the village that I believed was still there.

When I came back, it was once again in an old car. One neighboring friend had arranged for me to rent it from another. The crossroad where I had first turned onto the unpaved cart track to the village (at that time there had been no signpost at all, of course, and when I had left there had been a single board bearing only the name of the hamlet itself) was bedizened like the chest of a general with wooden panels painted in the maroon brown that had become the officially authentic color for rustic woodwork—much of which, in backward actuality, had gone unpainted or had been given an occasional coat of creosote manufactured down next to the railroad station. The placards, fresh, neat, and all of the same vintage, indicated the direction—and the distance, to the decimal of a kilometer—not only to every hamlet, *lieudit,* and large farm but to every hotel, restaurant, bed-and-breakfast, campsite, and swimming pool in four directions, with symbols referring to codes in tourist guidebooks.

I had left the village on an icy day, with snow and sleet falling, and on the way to the crossroad I had looked through the cold mist, along a familiar lane leading under half-bare walnut trees toward a friend's aging peach orchard and an empty house beyond it on a cliff jutting out over the valley. The field and plum trees next to the lane did not belong to my friend but to a neighbor with, as he had put it, a different mentality. Years later, when I drove back slowly from the crossroad at the end of summer, I saw that the old plum trees had been replaced by a yellowish industrial sheep barn constructed of undulated pressed sheeting. Across the road from it stood an inhabited but unfinished dwelling in textured stucco, with lawn ornaments. The road led on past one other recent, plain stone house in a traditional pattern, and as it turned at the ancient lane and the oak wood, the farm buildings that came into view, and the house, and the roofs of the village beyond them, did not appear to have changed at all.

It was still August. The wine harvest had not begun. A time of hushed, luminous days, kites sailing high over the slopes, an unbounded calm. Reunions with old friends. Talk of those who had died or gone away, and what had happened or was happening to their houses and to the village. In my years there before, every house had been inhabited by a farming family, or by the artisans, the roofer and the mason—except for the one lived in by a retired French diplomat and his learned wife, and the other one acquired some years later by a French professor of modern German literature. Now that was all over. An age had gone. A number of the pastures and one of the barns had been rented out to modernized farmers in neighboring hamlets. On the lane above the village one piece of wooded pasture after another had been sold and turned into a building lot. Barns at the edge of the village were about to become the property of English people with apparently unbounded means and the intention of turning them into showplaces with swimming pools in the barnyards, and name signs declaring that they were barns. At least, friends said, they had been able to prevent the building of a hotel, though there had been one Belgian millionaire who perhaps had not yet given up the idea. In what had been a farming village there were no animals any longer, except for a few fenced hens, one flock of sheep herded back and forth to the rented pastures by men in cars, and lapdogs on weekends.

But there were changes of another kind, relating to the past. As the life that had formed it ebbed away a surge of new interest in the language had emerged. It was being taught not only at the University of Toulouse but in the public schools, and in the village it was referred to not only as patois but sometimes, rather cautiously, as Occitan. There was no way to foresee the future of such a turn either there or elsewhere in the world, or of understanding all that it might represent, although theories of various kinds played over it. In the meantime, even in the Maison de la Presse in the small nearby market town, one could find reprints of several Occitan-French dictionaries, including Levy's *Petit Dictionnaire Provençal-Français,* as well as a few texts and anthologies of the troubadours, many reprints of regional material from cookbooks to accounts of the Knights Templar, and serious periodicals devoted to local archaeology, architecture, cultural and linguistic history. Whether this was a genuine resurgence or something less substantial, the renewed interest had led to historic discoveries.

I had remarried after I had left, all those years before, and my wife, who had never known the region, loved it at first sight. It was time to look at the whole place again.

That same year Daniel Halpern asked several poets to contribute translations of cantos of Dante's *Inferno* to a complete version of it. After years of translating I was thoroughly aware that it is an impossible undertaking, and I had lectured on the particular impossibilities of translating Dante. We persist in the enterprise not because it can be accomplished to anyone's final satisfaction but simply because it is necessary. Halpern persuaded me to see what I could do with two cantos of my own choosing. I tried to be as accurate as possible and still produce lines that could be read as a poem in English, and suggest the form and rhymes and above all the pace of the Italian without presenting a tortured replication of them.

The attempt led me to wonder what I could do with the section of the poem that I had always felt most drawn to, the *Purgatorio*. The arts, and especially poetry, singing, and poets, from Virgil to Guinizelli and the singer Casella, figure most fully, fondly, and intimately in this part of the work. I had lingered many times over the twenty-sixth canto, which above all is the one devoted to poets. It is the one from which Eliot's dedicatory phrase *il miglior fabbro* is taken. Far up on the mountain in the ring of fire, in that otherworldly gathering of Dante's poetic forebears, the circling canto leads back to the great troubadours, and to the one whom Dante regarded as supreme among them, Arnaut Daniel. At the end of the canto, when this opinion of Dante's has been expressed in a way that makes clear his familiarity with the corpus of troubadour literature (including much that has been lost since his time), Arnaut Daniel answers him not in Italian but in his own language, Occitan. The passage, which seems to me one of the most beautiful in the entire *Commedia,* echoes lines from Arnaut Daniel's most personal poem, one which in turn may carry deliberate echoes of his Arabic antecedents. The lines that Dante transforms are the culmination and signature of Arnaut Daniel's poem:

> *Ieu sui Arnaut qu'amas l'aura*
> *E chatz la lebre ab lo bou*
> *E nadi contra suberna.*

I am Arnaut who gather the wind
And ride the ox to hunt the hare
And I swim against the tide.

In the *Purgatorio,* he introduces himself with the line

Ieu sui Arnaut, que plor e vau cantan.

I am Arnaut, who weep and go singing.

As I was led back to the subject of the troubadours, and discovered a rich flowering of new work that had been produced within a generation, I learned more about the extent and depth of Dante's debt to those earlier poets, his mentors, and was reminded of the literary primacy of the Occitan language in his time, which was imposing enough to have raised the possibility of his writing his own poem not in Latin, as some would have expected, nor even in Italian, where the poetic tradition was just beginning, but in Occitan. His inheritance from the troubadours was complicated by their own various roles and histories in the great civilizing surge of Languedoc, the awakening that was the glory of the Counts of Toulouse, and was systematically plundered, razed, degraded, and half-obliterated by the tide of self-righteous predation known as the Albigensian Crusade, the immediate herald of the Inquisition. I returned to Dante's poem over the years in spite of the orthodox Christianity that prompted him to people his Paradise with such figures as Dominic and Folquet de Marseilla. The source of his central metaphor was deeper than doctrinal contortions, and the power of his best poetry has an authority not born of reason or theology. Arnaut's own words, behind Dante's in the twenty-sixth canto of the *Purgatorio,* made me want to try again to hear something of the troubadours' brief, bright sense of the world. To find what ruins, indeed, might still be standing.

Of all the troubadours, there was none whose poems I loved more than those of Bernart de Ventadorn.

CHAPTER FIVE

Tucked into the upper right-hand corner of the Michelin map of France #75, just east of the small town of Égletons, in the mountainous *département* of the Corrèze, a triangle of black dots near the village of Moustier-Ventadour indicates the ruins of the château. Égletons is only about an hour's drive from the old farmhouse, and in earlier years I had asked residents of the region about the ruins, but had been left with the impression that there was not much there but a pile of stones off in the thickets. No one to whom I had spoken had seemed to know much about them. This time, as close to them as the town of Égletons itself, it took a chain of inquiries to produce a serious young woman in an empty tourist office, surrounded by posters of summer music festivals in famous places, who gave me—with many disclaimers about its being entirely unofficial—a mimeographed reproduction of a hand-drawn map, and a sketch of the château (made, she confessed, by herself) as no one living, and perhaps no one ever, had seen it. In a confidential tone she said to me that most of the few who inquired about the château were foreigners. And with some hesitation she provided me with the address of a man of letters, Luc de Goustine, living a few kilometers from the ruins, whom I arranged to meet, and who turned out to know more about the place and its history than I could have hoped to discover.

The forests north of Égletons are not the towering primal wilderness that reigned there between the last ice age and the deforestation that picked up speed in the late Middle Ages. The great trees went long ago, but there are later, less imperial forests cloaking the mountains. In high spring, with the birches and chestnuts in their first full green and the new grass tall along the highway that was still innocent of summer traffic, only the shyest of markers indicated where we should double back from the *Route Nationale* to reach Moustier-Ventadour. The smaller road, winding between verges of bracken and broom, emerged, turn by turn, out of hiding. Swaybacked lengths of old fence, and vagrant hedgerows, and undergrowth returning to woods. Late morning. Rain light with sunny patches in which the yellow broom flowers, the *genêt*, glistened.

It is said that in the early years of the twelfth century, in the days when the first ramparts of the château had just been built, Geoffrey the Fair, Count of Anjou, liked to decorate his helmet with sprigs of genêt, and so came to be known as Geoffrey Plantagenet, and the name was passed on to his son Henry, who would become King of England, Henry II, the first of the line of Plantagenet kings.

Remnants of woodpiles, dark at the end of winter, survived at the edges of woods. Oaks, cornels, and here and there the snow of hawthorns, the may trees, in their flowering month for which, in England, they are named. For a moment my wife and I were not even certain that we were on the right road. Then we came to the gray wall enclosing a cemetery, and rounding a bend saw the backs of farm buildings and houses. A spreading tree with a round table under it, near the road, and propped under a front window a sign that looked like a relic itself, with large letters on white-painted planks, promising *Antiquités*. Graying lace like cobwebs clouded the window above it, and a smiling woman with white hair, setting a chair at the round table, waved to us as we went by on our way to Moustier. But that was Moustier—more or less the center of the village. There was the World War I monument, the staring helmeted soldier, slightly smaller than life-size, with the engraved names below, a list that must have been far longer than the latest census of the commune. There was no one else in sight.

From the house by the old tree the larger of two lanes curved to the right, and on its left a small, plain church with Romanesque lines stood back from the roadway. Then came a few houses among trees—farmhouses, some with long grass growing up to their doors. At what seemed to be the end of the village there was one working farm, the mud of a barnyard, a small family of machinery, one cow barn evidently in use. But the noon hour was approaching and the village had withdrawn under its roofs, except for the dogs barking behind one iron gate near the church. Not farm dogs but hunting dogs, noisy and friendly. A number of the houses in the village appeared not to be farm dwellings any longer but were perhaps inhabited by people who had retired from farming, or they may have become the country places of families in Égletons or Tulle or Ussel.

The name Moustier, an old word for minster or monastery, had suggested to me a building of considerable size, reminding me of a line of Middle English in which being adrift in vast and cavernous space is conveyed by the image of "a mote in a minster door." I had assumed that the church at the center of the village was a chapel or subsidiary of the main compound nearby, which would be an impressive, probably fortified, relic. But the plain structure, scarcely larger than the neighboring houses, with its graceful but unremarkable arched doorway, proved to be all that remained of the *moustier*. Its façade, I learned later from Luc de Goustine, was a reconstruction dating from the seventeenth century. Whatever bits of original masonry were still part of it had survived from the monastery or priory built in the years just before 1116, in the hamlet then known as Drulle, or Oak Forest. Relics of Gaulish houses and of buildings from the time of the Roman occupation have been found near springs in the woods. There are Neolithic standing stones and undated burial sites not far from the area that was chosen for the monastery during the generation or so following the preliminary leveling of the top of the rough crag of Ventadorn and the construction of the first tower and walls in the shape of a great stone ship up there.

The feudal lord under whose command the original château was built was Viscount Eble I. His son and heir, Eble II, the Singer, was one of the earliest troubadours. None of his poems has survived, but it was he who was responsible for the building of the moustier. He may have been prompted by pure piety, as has been claimed. In his youth, in 1109, he gave a farm to the abbey of Tulle, and thirty-eight years later he, and his son who would become Eble III, took part in the unsuccessful Second Crusade, in 1147, where legend has it that his incendiary verses were sung beneath the walls of Damascus to urge on the besieging crusaders. According to one account he died on the way back, at Monte Cassino, and was buried there.

But whatever Eble II's orthodox fervor may have led him to, a domain such as the Viscount of Ventadorn's, in the early twelfth century, would have included assorted dependencies of the church, representatives of ecclesiastical power, to allow for the observance of the religious calendar and the sacraments, and to provide sanctified places for burial. The small priory at Moustier was staffed with five or six monks under the orders of the Abbey of Cluny.

Through the first half of the twelfth century, the fervor of Christendom in France radiated from the figure of Bernard de Clairvaux, the zealous ascetic, "the hawk of Rome." In one of his letters the abbot refers to himself as being related to the family of Guilhem de Peitau. He also claimed to abhor violence, but in the interests of the church he managed to approve, and then to exhort with inflammatory sermons, the massing of the Second Crusade, and the unassailable self-righteousness of his language and of his mind proved to be a magma of carnage and destruction.

Probably the eminent abbot himself never journeyed to the priory at Moustier-Ventadorn, but almost certainly his words did. He was famous for his torrents of incendiary rhetoric, denouncing every pleasure that he could imagine, every fondness for the living world. His homilies were copied in whole or in part, and repeated in various accents across the country. His periods inciting the listening provincials to the hatreds and advantages of a holy war almost as far away from them as the courts of heaven may have echoed under the roof of the moustier, some of whose builders, perhaps, were still alive, standing inside or outside the door. The burning words would have been distinct, up near the pulpit, to Viscount Eble II, whose "school" of poetry and chivalry would hardly have gained the grim abbot's approval—and to the viscount's family. And perhaps to Bernart de Ventadorn, still a boy at the time and—depending on which account of his life may be closest to the truth—either listening with members of the viscount's family, up near the font where he had been christened a few years earlier, or catching the odd word while standing outside among the villeins and servants, in the unheeding weather and birdsong.

But only the name of the place, the site, and some of the stones are still the same. If the listeners stood there again today they would not recognize much. The church they knew rose within defensive battlements and extended into a complex of cloisters, cells, main hall, refectory, kitchen, all of which have vanished. The heavy Romanesque arches collapsed, in the course of the first three centuries, and were rebuilt three years after the first voyage of Columbus. And there were extensive restorations, financed in part by offerings from the parish, during the years just before the French Revolution, and again during the nineteenth century. But they came after periods of neglect and dilapidation, when much of the original compound had fallen and been taken away. The door to what is there now was locked.

The other lane, from the round table by the tree, and the windows full of gray lace, led downhill past gates of stone cottages with more lace in the windows, cats sleeping on woodpiles, a ruined barn, two donkeys in the woods, one working farm with new hay rakes out in the barnyard for the first haying. Their wheels of yellow spokes were raised as though in homage to the sun, and stood there motionless in the sacred French noon hour while everyone was indoors at table. From out in the lane we could hear the clink of plates through the notes of chaffinches and blackbirds. Beyond the sunbursts of the hay rakes we could see, at the top of the ridge on the far side of the small valley, the towering shells and shards of high walls the color of the lace in the windows: The profile of what was there of the château nine hundred and fifty years after its first stones were set in place. A few steps below the farm we began to hear the rushing of water somewhere in the hidden ravine ahead of us.

In the farm walls along the lane, among the sloe bushes and brambles, remnants of what I thought might be other masonry appeared to be half-buried: larger stones, some of them cut and fitted more tightly than the walls around them. At one time the outer ring of fortifications extended from the foot of the castle to the approaches on the slopes around it. The moving of stones is the course of history, and of rubble and forgetting. In its great days in the twelfth and thirteenth centuries, when the castle was still called Ventadorn, it—along with several others in the region such as the Tours de Merle and Turenne—was said to be impregnable, and perhaps, at least until the common use of artillery, they all were. But as late as the seventeenth century Louis-Charles de Lévis, then the Duke of Ventadour and a Peer of France (though he was hunchbacked, which interfered with a military career, and had a reputation as a libertine, which annoyed the king) could boast to Louis XIV, "Sire, all the straw of your kingdom could not fill the moats of our château." He had in mind, no doubt, the situation of Ventadour, high on its cliff above the deep gorges of the Soudeillette and the Vigne, whose roaring torrents we could hear but not see. But his words sound like a reiteration of a family assurance regarding the château, a saying that may have passed down through generations, lingering more than a century after the heirs had ceased to occupy Ventadour. It was the kind of persistent attitude that made Richelieu, during the same period, want to destroy every *château fort* in France that might be capable of resisting his dreams of control. Fortunately he died before his demolition projects had reached the great castles of the Corrèze and the Quercy. But in the generations after the duke's boast the family's concern for the château dissipated. They had a summer residence and hunting lodge at Davignac, and a château at Peyroux where they stayed much of the time when the heads of the family were not away on military campaigns, or at court with the king—and Louis XIV preferred to keep the heads of powerful families close to him, to attenuate their attachments to their own domains.

During those years, for two centuries while a domestic staff continued to reside at Ventadour, a member of the gentry, a castellan or governor, remained in charge, until 1789 and the revolution. Combarel de Gebanel was the name of the last one on the records. But before his tenure, in 1783, a judge from the *châtellenie* of Égletons, M. d'Ambert de Gerilhac, learned that stones were being sold "from the debris of the château" at Ventadour, and he sent a petition to the current head of the family, the Prince de Soubise, in Paris, asking to buy the fifteenth century tympanum depicting Samson killing a lion, from the top of a wall between the ramparts and the main courtyard. His bid was accepted, upon condition that the removal of the relief did not damage the wall. The prince, it may be noted, had been born in Paris sixty-eight years earlier, and would die there four years later. Whether or not he had ever visited Ventadour in the course of his life, he may not have been aware of the condition of the castle by the time he agreed to the removal of the Samson bas-relief. The fact that there was already "debris" being sold suggests that dilapidation, by that time, was well advanced.

Quantities of stones were probably carted off during the revolution and might now be part of any of the buildings we had passed. In the summer of 1796 (21 messidor, year IV), the château with its farms and enclosures was sold to a farrier in Égletons named Antoine Estrade for the sum of twelve thousand francs. He was a native of Rouergue but was currently living in the manor house of Rebeyrotte, in the nearby commune of Sarran, a fortified building with towers. Apparently he kept the château, debris and all, as it was, for a while, but he was not making anything on his twelve thousand francs, and it was sure to cost him more, even if he did nothing with it. He sold it for fourteen thousand francs to a person with the resounding name of Ignace Perthuis du Roussillon et du Gay, who knew exactly what he wanted to do with his investment. At the time of the purchase he was deep in debt, but the remains of the château were there to save him. Whether or not he had ever heard of

Louis-Charles de Lévis' boast to Louis XIV, about all the straw in France and the moats at Ventadour, it did not trouble his calculations. He managed to fill in an approach to the cliff on the side toward the village, and then build a new road across it and up around the walls, where he opened a large passage for wagons to take out the dressed stones. In the year that Napoleon returned from Elba and summoned his remaining followers for the campaign that ended at Waterloo, Ignace Perthuis du Roussillon et du Gay began his systematic dismantling of the château of Ventadour.

He managed to sell off most of the carved stone ornaments, facings, embrasures of the walls, the crenellations of the towers and ramparts, the stone door lintels and window frames, fixtures and adornments from the living quarters, halls, chapels, and outer rooms. The Samson-and-the-lion motif may have been repeated in a number of panels. One, now in a house in Égletons, bears the motto *"Dura, duris frango":* "Strong, I break the strong." Other panels from Ventadour with reliefs of heraldic devices are now in various buildings in Égletons. A fifteenth-century stone doorway and a window above, from the château's living quarters, are part of the presbytery there, and a matching window has been identified on a house along the road to Soudeilles. Two carved doorposts and a number of steps of a spiral staircase are in a barn near Moustier. At Forgeix, not far from there, a carved lintel has been set above the door of a sheep barn, and six windows from one floor of the living quarters were transported to the commune of Laval-sur-Luzège, where M. Perthuis du Roussillon et du Gay was living at the time of his enterprise. When M. Perthuis du Roussillon et du Gay suspended his operations, the remains stood as a monument to his vision for the rest of the century, with brambles growing in the mortar of the walls and saplings in the courtyards, until the danger of stones falling from the derelict fortifications and rolling down across the cart track prompted the authorities, in 1906, to order a mason in Moustier to lower still farther the crumbling walls of the round tower and some of the ramparts.

That ironic public project of protecting the neighborhood by lowering the walls that had been built to defend it was carried out at a time when the valleys and hamlets around Ventadour had been sinking into the kind of sleep we are told of in children's stories. In those same years, the last decades of the nineteenth century, and then those just before the First World War, serious studies of the troubadours and their civilization were being carried out by a number of great scholars, French, German, English, Italian, and Spanish, who cooperated with each other on what must have seemed to them a singularly peaceful enterprise in an age of singular peace.

For Carl Appel, the pioneer in the work on Bernart de Ventadorn, that peace must have seemed to be epitomized by the somnolence of the ruins of the château and of their setting as he found them in the early years of the twentieth century When he came to publish his *Introduction to Bernart de Ventadorn,* in Breslau, it was 1915, and he prefaced it with a grief-stricken foreword looking back to the friendship of those earlier years. Much of the preparation of the volume had been completed, he said, as the clouds of war gathered above the place where he lived. How ridiculous the tinkling of the medieval poet's lyre sounded in the midst of the roar of modern weapons, and how ridiculous the quest of a scholar of languages for some minute fragment of truth at a time when a storm of lies was sweeping the planet. In the realm of Romance philology, perhaps more than in any other, German and French scholars had always worked hand in hand, but now it seemed that among French scholars the hatred of Germany was more pronounced than almost anywhere. It had been his intention, he wrote, to dedicate his work to the French and English friends with whom he had passed peaceful days wandering through the troubadour's native countryside, but it was not the moment, then, to importune them publicly with assurances of his profound esteem, or of the unbroken friendship that he continued to feel for them, whose expression could only compromise them in their own countries.

Appel's description of the region around Ventadour, and the approach to the ruins, as he remembered them some time later in another country during that war, is an evocation of an enchanted forest. He was almost sixty at the time when he wrote his foreword, and even if it had not been long since he had last seen it, the landscape he was remembering, as well as whatever had brought him to the language and poems of Bernart, belonged to his youth. He speaks of the region unequivocally as the place of origin of the poetry of the troubadours, the country that the first generations of them thought of as the homeland of their art.

For his visit or visits in search of their past he had taken the train from Brive, which had puffed along at top speed to the stop at Égletons, and he had walked on from there. The tenderness with which he recalls that country is colored by his grief, for it represents a great deal that is beyond him now, and by the helpless nostalgia that pervades so much that comes to us from his generation and the time of the fin de siècle and the years before the first war, a tone of regret and longing that recurs insistently in the wake of the high surge of nineteenth-century Romanticism. It inherits from the Romantics and their own origins a century earlier, from fairy tales and Gothic fantasy, the lure of the high Middle Ages, a time imperfectly defined, forever out of reach, its smells and its sufferings as remote as tapestries, an era whose attraction was enhanced by the impossibility of ever being part of it.

If he had approached the château in Bernart's day, Appel would no doubt have been horrified by the cruelties around him, but he arrived there when the rawness of that age was gone, and the carved glories of the château after it, and it could seem to him a place of tranquility. Nothing, he wrote, could be more agreeable to the senses than the walk along the ridge above the Limousin valleys, the hills rolling away like long waves, a well-kept country lane—and he interrupted himself to allow an English writer, perhaps one of the friends of whom he had spoken in the foreword, with whom he had visited the region, to take up the portrayal of the place as Appel himself had seen it.

Appel's decision, and the passages he cites at length from a book by Justin H. Smith, *Troubadours At Home,* reveals something about Appel himself and the tastes that he must have shared with others of his generation. The saccharine prose depicts a scene on a period chocolate box or something out of Victorian children's books, more appropriate to the revived vogue of the ballade fostered by G. K. Chesterton and his friends than to the troubadours. Yet Smith's histrionic enthusiasm for the approach to Ventadour—the lane on which my wife and I were walking—was obviously genuine, and it conveyed details of the place in the early years of the twentieth century. The winding variety of the lane filled him with admiration: neat fences, open fields, banks above eye level, hollows falling away. The blackthorn (sloe) alternating with the whitethorn (the hawthorn, or may). A survey of the trees. Hemp growing in the fields, as it did wherever sheep were raised and wool was spun in the region. The juxtaposition of tidy husbandry and tumbling anarchy, which plainly did not look at all like England. The houses at the corner by the church, and down along the lane, had thatched roofs reaching almost to the ground, with dormers set into them like nests, grapevines in a roof gutter, wildflowers everywhere, and birdsong, and birds. Mr. Smith declared the cart track to Ventadour to be unquestionably the best of all country lanes.

The ruined château, when he—or they—reached it on its spur, was half-buried in thickets and trees. Ivy and thornbushes grew over and out of the walls. Much of that growth has since been removed or cut back. In 1963 the owners of the château were given a grant by the beaux-arts commission, toward the preservation of the remains, and other contributions from concerns in the area have helped in the work and in the archaeological exploration of the site. When we reached there, even the place that Appel and Smith had seen was already beyond living memory.

When they saw the ruins, the site belonged to a collateral descendant of the family of Ventadour, who had bought it in the

1890s. In 1988 one of his heirs gave it to the commune of Moustier-Ventadour, which is now in charge of the site and the use of it.

Now the lane widens at the foot of the slope, with a scuffed, bare turnaround for trucks and machinery used in the current works in progress. A wooden toolshed beside it, a single small cubicle. A sign outside announced postcards for sale, but May was not the season, and the door was locked. We were alone with the ruins. On a pedestal by the lane, a glass plaque is engraved with lines from a poem by Bernart de Ventadorn and lines by Maria de Ventadorn, and a caption: "These stones saw them live. In these lines they live again."

The truck road leading up the side of the hill to what Appel thought was the original entrance was really the construction that the enterprising M. Perthuis du Roussillon et du Gay had engineered at the end of the Napoleonic era, to allow him to gut the château as though it were a quarry. The real entrance was at a lower level: an arched portal facing us, just where the rise began, with a series of shallow steps ascending under vaults, through the walls. Part of the vaulting of the roof had collapsed before Appel's visit, burying the passage, which was not reopened until 1988. Now one can climb up into the first court-yard and enter it the way Eble II, the Singer, and his wife Agnes de Monluçon, and Bernart did, and stand at the top among bare wreckage they could scarcely have imagined.

Stones lie wherever they are as though they had always been there and would always stay there. Our awareness of our own pace in time keeps us from recognizing that the motions of stones are akin to those of snowflakes and molecules, and to us the moment in which they lie seems like an unchanging condition, and they come to exemplify permanence. So the Venus de Milo looks to us as though she had never had arms at all, and the ruin appears to have been the truth of the château from the beginning.

CHAPTER SIX

It was Bernart, and not Bernart himself but his poems, that had
first made me want to come there, to stand there, just as they
had brought Carl Appel almost a century before. But Appel had
been a scholar of Romance languages, of Occitan and the surviving texts and traditions of the troubadours, for some time
before he first got off the train at Égletons. What he could know
then about the history of the château had great gaps in it like the
walls themselves, but he had been able to study the clues to
Bernart's life, such as they were, and to arrive at a coherent, if
not absolute assessment of them.

When I first sailed for Europe, on the day of General
Douglas MacArthur's triumphal parade in New York, the poems
and the *vida* in my one anthology of troubadour poetry were all
I had with me about Bernart de Ventadorn.

The account of his life that I deciphered there was in fact

one of several versions. One of them asserted that the statements were the work of a later troubadour, Uc de Saint-Circ; and the author, whether Uc or someone else claiming to be him, declared that all this had been told him by Count Eble de Ventadorn, "who was the son of the viscountess with whom Bernart had been so much in love." The summary, whatever truth there may be in it, is the basis for most of the later legend about Bernart.

It says that he was from the Limousin, from the castle of Ventadorn, and that he was of humble origin, the son of a baker who stoked the oven to bake the bread for the château. He grew up to be handsome and intelligent, with a gift for composing poems and for singing, and he was courteous and learned. He and his poems gave great pleasure to the Viscount of Ventadorn, who showed him great honor. The viscount's wife was beautiful, high-spirited, young and noble. She found Bernart and his songs attractive and she fell in love with him, and he with her. So he wrote his poems and his songs about her and his love for her, and how admirable she was.

Their love went on for a long time before the viscount and the people in the castle discovered it. And when the viscount learned of it he sent Bernart away and had his wife locked up under guard. So the lady released Bernart and sent to tell him to leave the region. And he left, and went to the Duchess of Normandy, who was young and of great nobility, with a great liking for merit and honor and songs in praise of her. Bernart's verses and songs gave her great pleasure, and she welcomed him, honored him, encouraged him, and heaped favors upon him. He stayed a long time at the court of the duchess and fell in love with her, and she with him, and Bernart made many fine songs for her.

But King Henry of England took her for his wife, and carried her away from Normandy to England, and Bernart remained back here, sad and grieving. He left Normandy and went to the good Count of Toulouse, and remained at his court until the count's death. And when the count died, Bernart left the world, and the making of poems, and singing, and the pleasures of earthly life, and entered the order of Dalon and ended his days that way.

It is a good story, and an example of why the vidas have a place among the earliest romances, and have contributed to the making of the word *romance* itself. The Duchess of Normandy was, of course, Aliénor (or as she is known now, Eleanor) of Aquitaine. She was divorced from the King of France, Louis VII, in 1152, and married to Henry Plantagenet barely eight weeks later. Among her titles was that of Duchess of Normandy, and she resided and held court in Normandy at several periods of her life, but the vida is not a reliable indication of just when and where the relations between Bernart and Aliénor developed, or what, besides the poems, they amounted to. Carl Appel cast a sharp eye over such clues as he thought were worth trying to follow, and he arranged them tentatively in accord with the known chronology.

Appel believed that Bernart was born between 1120 and 1130. The date of his death is not certain either, but it is not likely that it was very long after 1200. The Viscountess of Ventadorn with whom, according to the vida, Bernart was first in love, could have been the wife of Eble III. But which wife? The viscount was married twice, first to Marguerite de Turenne, who died in 1148. She would have been the viscountess at the time of Bernart's youth. However, Count Eble IV of Ventadorn, whom the vida cites as the authority for the story, was not her son but the child of Eble III's second wife, Alaiz de Montpelier. It seems unlikely that Bernart could have been in love with Alaiz, whom Eble III did not marry until 1151, the year before Bernart, if that part of the story is to be believed, would most probably have left for Normandy.

Decades must have passed between Bernart's death and the time when Uc, or whoever was using his name, wrote the vida. Eble IV would have been in his seventies or older, and we are invited to believe that the viscount at that age would have confided morsels of his mother's love life to a minstrel with a somewhat dubious local reputation, or to someone even less reliable who would invoke both their names in order to seem credible. What Uc, or some copier using his name, was purveying may have been nothing more, in some passages, than bits of gossip passed on repeatedly by the time they were assembled and recited as introductions, and finally written down.

Most of the vidas, perhaps all of them, apparently came into existence in the same way, compiled by itinerant minstrels, jongleurs, in order to have something to say about the poets whose verses they were about to sing—poets whom they had never met, about whom they knew, in fact, little or nothing, and who in most cases were no longer living. Their purpose, in most cases, evidently was not to provide accurate information but to catch the attention of the audience before performances of the songs. The earliest printed versions were made in Italy in the thirteenth century, perhaps by refugees from the Albigensian Crusade. Some details of the vidas and of the slightly later *razos,* or conventionalized commentaries, seem to have been extrapolated out of lines in the poems themselves.

Having said that as a reminder not to take the historical accuracy of the vidas for granted, something should be said about Uc de Saint-Circ, the thirteenth-century troubadour who is credited with compiling a large number of them, Bernart's among them. In the classic modern edition of the vidas and razos by Jean Boutière and A. H. Schutz in 1949, the only two authors to whose names any of the texts were attributed were Miquel de la Tor and Uc de Saint-Circ, who was, the editors say, "effectively a jongleur." Apparently he was one of the itinerant minstrels of his time who lived along the precarious border between the status of jongleur—which ranked socially with jugglers, acrobats, animal acts, and prostitutes—and troubadours. And as we know, the troubadours whose songs the jongleurs sang were often members of the nobility.

The Boutière and Schutz edition of the vidas includes three distinct "lives" of Uc, describing different periods, and three love affairs. And though the first of these tells of him leaving his studies with the priests in Montpelier to become a jongleur, the space and detail accorded to his story (even if he wrote it himself) suggest someone whose gifts, learning, and originality went far beyond the ordinary, even though much of his existence must have been unstable and uncertain, and there were apparently times when he was penniless, with no fixed place of abode, and—as the local saying went—had to eat pig's snout.

In the years when Appel was working on Bernart's poems, the great French Occitan scholar Alfred Jeanroy and J. J. Salverda de Grave were editing the poems of Uc de Saint-Circ. At least

forty of those have survived—a high number for any troubadour—and they too make it plain that although Uc may have
lived as a jongleur at various times, driven to it by luck or the
restlessness of his own nature, he was certainly a troubadour, and
a gifted one.

Another thread, from closer to home, drew me before I knew it
toward this mercurial, talented, motley figure who in the end
had been responsible for so much of the gossip and extrapolation
that came to be handed down as biographical fact about Bernart
and about many of the troubadours.

After I moved to the house in the village, for most of two
decades I spent days exploring on foot the vast uninhabited
upland, the *causse,* that began just above the last farmhouse, a
few minutes' walk from my own. The rolling landscape is a
limestone plateau, the undulating roof covering a vast complex
of crevices, caves, caverns, subterranean rivers that wind far
underground and emerge at last as waterfalls or springs flowing
into the Dordogne. On the ridges and open barrens a thin layer
of rocky soil covers the white stone. The earth is darker and richer in the hollows, and the vegetation is greener there in summer.
Oak woods rise along the slopes.

In that region the causses extend from the cliffs above one
great river valley to the cliffs above the next one, and they
determine the whole character of the place, a huge, vibrant
silence, which I discovered like an unimagined legacy in the
lengthening days of spring, the cicada-tremolo of summer, the
mists and elegiac tones of autumn, and the opening perspec-

tives of winter, as the leaves fell and the dark branches stood out against the brief snows.

The causse there had once sustained a population of scattered farms, but the population dwindled through the nineteenth century and then fell away sharply during World War I, when so many young men from the region were called to the armies in the north and never came back. The old lanes still led across the upland between ancient walls. The passage of flocks of sheep and of cows during the dry summer months kept them open for some distance from the villages, and there were sheep barns, far out at the edges of woods, that were still in use for folding small flocks. There were also many abandoned stone houses and barns (sometimes they occupied opposite ends of the same building) in various stages of dissolution. Some still had most of their roofs and some of their beams, but trees were growing up from the floor below. Some, it seemed, were part of an earlier generation, roofless long since, their walls sinking back into the woods. Some were all but hidden under brambles and ivy.

There were other ruins, besides, of ancient fortifications, and about some of those I learned fragments of history or legend. I bought the appropriate *État Major* maps of the area (1 cm to 250 m), the French equivalent of American geodetic survey maps, and pored over them. They were long, rather fragile rolls of paper and I did not fold them to carry with me, but studied them after hours of walking. In theory, they showed every building on the causse that was standing at the date when an edition of the map was made. On older editions, houses and farms that I knew as ruins, and others that I had not found at all, appeared as contemporaries with all the others, and there were names I had never heard written across hills and hollows.

From a friend who was leaving the region I bought a Vespa, which allowed me to extend the range of my explorations. I could put-put at nearly a walking pace, up a sheep track on the causse until I could go no farther, and then leave the bike locked under a bush and set out on foot. I carried binoculars for birds, a field guide for wildflowers, and the lure of the land and its past led me on. After years in all seasons I felt that I had barely had a glimpse of it.

More than once, beyond Thégra and Gramat, I followed a lane to a stick signpost pointing into a thicket above a steep overgrown path that snaked down into a gorge, and led to the Moulin du Saut: ruined stone rooms built into the overhanging cliff, descending through each other, over the main flow of the stream. It was one of a series of mills in the narrow echoing canyon of the Alzou between Roumégouse and Rocamadour. The small but powerful torrent curled and twisted around the base of a promontory, a tableland crested with oak woods, the Bois de la Pannonie, and at the edge of the woods, by a few old farm buildings, the map told of the ruins of a château. I could see little there but jumbled stones, but the spot seemed even more secret than the country around it. I knew a few details about the mills deep along the Alzou, but nothing for some time about the past of the stony barren near the woods on the promontory above.

The year after I shook hands with the woman in Miers and became the next owner of the long-uninhabited farmhouse overlooking the river, another farmhouse, which I had been shown at first, at the bottom of the village, was bought by a French diplomat, who had held a consular post in North Africa. In due course I met my neighbors but we never got to know each other very well.

It was only after I had returned to the village, and after my neighbor's wife, Mme. Jacquette Luquet-Juillet, had died, that I learned from her husband of Mme. Juillet's work, all those years, on a four-volume study of Occitan culture, literature, and society in the age of the troubadours. In the course of it she had written an authoritative essay on Uc de Saint-Circ, who had come from our own area, almost from the village. Her husband gave me her monograph on Uc, published in the *Bulletin de la Société des Études du Lot* during the years when I was away. I learned from it that Uc's family had once lived on the plateau above the Moulin du Saut where I had stood wondering about the site, probably at about the same time that she was unearthing what facts remained about it. Both of us, through those years, had looked down from the village to the great red château of Castelnau-Bretenoux, on a spur in the valley, where Uc evidently found shelter and patronage at one point in his life.

The first of the vidas about Uc seems to contradict itself about where he was born, saying that it was at a castle "at the foot of" Rocamadour, and in the *bor*, or town, of Thégra. But J. A. Delpon, in *Statistique du Département du Lot* in 1831, wrote about the location of the castle of Saint-Circ, "since ruined by wars and calamities" (as one of the vidas about Uc says), where Uc's father, Armand, was a (perhaps landless) vavasor, a member of the lesser nobility who was a kind of majordomo there. The château occupied the high promontory that falls away on three sides in stony cliffs, above a loop of the narrow river Alzou, the place near the Bois de la Pannonie that I remembered, and it was a site with a long human past even in Uc's time. In the ruins and around them, in the early nineteenth century, the remains of former habitations were continually being discovered, and tombs, tools, bolts, Roman medals and coins dating back to the time of Trajan.

The château had been destroyed, perhaps by Henri Court-Mantel (the friend of Bertran de Born, who wrote a famous elegy at his death), which forced Uc's family to move to Thégra, a part of the same domain, and Uc was born there.

Delpon's investigations revealed that an enterprising person with no money to speak of had managed to buy the site at about the same time that Ignace Perthuis du Roussillon et du Gay bought Ventadour, and had sold it after a few years and bought "a considerable property," his fortunes having been greatly improved, apparently, by what he dug up in the ruins and took to Bordeaux—there are records of that—and sold there. The ancient church at Saint-Circ had been endowed, in the twelfth century, by a family related by marriage to Valon de Thégra. The ties between the two places may account for the statement that Uc had come from Saint-Circ and from Thégra.

Uc, according to the vida, ran off to be a jongleur near the end of the twelfth or the beginning of the thirteenth century. That would have been ten, twenty, perhaps thirty years after the death of Bernart, and on the eve of the Albigensian slaughters. For some time he found a patron in Savaric de Mauléon, son of a favorite of Henry II Plantagenet, and an enthusiastic host and supporter of troubadours. There are three vidas, of Savaric, at least one of them written, so the text says, by Uc, who boasts that he also carried a letter from Savaric to his lady. Uc wrote poems to a number of the grandes dames of the region, including Maria de Ventadorn.

He had a different sort of relation, acrimonious and impertinent, with the powerful Raimon III of Turenne, Maria de Ventadorn's brother. The source of the rancor between them, which sounds genuine, is unclear. In an exchange of verses, Uc says, "Sire, you forget your bragging when you fell asleep, but no lord is respected who cannot measure up to his boasts," and Raimon says, "You were sent to me in order to spy into my affairs, but I caught you." Uc's audacity, and Raimon's statement that he had been spying, both suggest that Uc had, and may have been acting for, a protector, possibly Gerbert de Castelnau-Gramat. (There was a power struggle between the lords of Turenne and those of Castelnau, whose domain included Thégra, and who were generous and consistent patrons of troubadours. The château library at Castelnau, in the seventeenth century, contained thirty-four folio volumes of the troubadours' poems.)

Later patrons of Uc's included the Count of Rodez, until he left for the Crusades, and Alfonso VIII of Castile, Alfonso IV of Léon, and Pedro II of Aragón. Around 1218-1219 he passed through Provence and seems to have visited the Countess Beatrice of Provence and Raimon des Baux. In 1220 he left the Languedoc altogether for Italy, and some three years later he married a lady in Treviso. Then for a while he was a guest at the court of Alberto Malaspina at Auramala, a family known for its literary patronage, and praised by Dante. He was a guest at the court of Ezzelino III da Romano, whose brother Alberico compiled the first anthology of Provençal poems—his own favorites—and of a succession of other Italian courts. He met Sordello, and the vida in Occitan portrays a markedly different figure from Dante's: not a brooding, leonine, aloof personage but an adventurous rake.

The vidas tell us that Uc himself wrote excellent love poems, but "after he had a wife he wrote no more of those." The first of the vidas about him (and it does seem probable that he was the author of most, and perhaps all of them) says that, fine though the poems were, he was not in love with any of the ladies he addressed them to, but that he was very skillful at expressing himself in the language of love.

It is now generally considered unlikely that he wrote the vida of Bernart that claims him as its author, and that story may have been composed at a date some time after Uc's own writings.

In the vida of Bernart that claims Uc as its author many things are questionable. Bernart's early love affair with the viscountess of Ventadorn, for one, although it may have had some basis in fact even if it reached the author, or authors, years later in the form of often repeated gossip. Another is the account of Bernart's humble origin.

The principal author of the vidas of Bernart, if he was a jongleur in the first half of the thirteenth century, probably had in his repertoire a sirventes, or satiric poem, by Peire d'Alvernhe, written, it is believed, in the spring of 1173, half a century before the compilation of many of the biographical forewords. Peire's poem had been composed for a gathering of twelve troubadours at Puivert, in the foothills of the Pyrénées. Luc de Goustine suggests that the banquet was a farewell from his poet friends to the troubadour Raimbaut d'Aurenga, who was known to be dying. The poem is a roasting of the company of old friends, one by one, with a stanza for each, and each stanza, while apparently speaking dismissively of them and their works and their reputations, alludes in terms that everyone there would have recognized, and presumably would have found amusing, to their distinctive talents, their characters and the most generally known characteristics of their lives.

Bernart is the third poet to whom Peire turns, after Giraud de Bornelh, and the stanza—on the face of it—runs:

The third, Bernart de Ventadorn,
is smaller than Bornelh by a hand,
his father a good serving man
who always bore the laburnum bow,
and his mother heated the oven
and bundled up the young shoots of the vine.

The author of the surviving vidas of Bernart evidently took the lines as a statement of fact, which would have been of slight interest to the assembled company, all of whom no doubt had known Bernart for years. The joke about size or status in the second line escapes us because we cannot know whether it alludes to some obvious physical difference, of the kind that led cowboys occasionally to dub tall men "Shorty," or whether it refers to some familiar turn of vanity or reputation. Bornelh, of whom he had just sung, was one of the most famous and most highly praised troubadours at the time—his vida called him "the master of the troubadours"—and Peire's poem says he is

like a goat skin bottle in the sun,
with a thin painful song
like the cry of the old water-bucket woman.

Bernart is the only troubadour in Peire's poem whose family background is mentioned, and his reference to it takes up most of the stanza. Unless we too take the references to Bernart's parents as plain history we can only guess at what Peire is alluding to, but it was something that everyone there knew all about. Are we really to suppose that the good serving man always bearing the laburnum bow was some man-at-arms at the castle? Why a laburnum bow, when other kinds of wood more generally used for bows were readily available? Ventadorn rhymes with *dorn* (handsbreadth, or fist), and *alborn* (laburnum), and *forn* (oven), and though the rhymes may have been part of the joke it seems unlikely that they accounted for all of it. Boughs of flowering laburnum in spring may have made bowers for covert trysts—anything of the kind is possible—but the subject of origins includes an erotic past, and the serving man never without his bow may be an allusion, among other things, to the god of love himself, and to a readiness other than military by someone who is to remain unnamed either because of his humble origin or, on the contrary, because of his "service" in a love affair within the circle of the viscount's family, or of his friends, which was a well-known secret.

Peire's tone was intended to tease but not to wound his friends and guests, and although the myths of chivalry embraced the notion that nobility attained was more worthy of admiration than nobility inherited, the notion was in great part fantasy, and tended to operate within somewhat restricted social circumstances. By the time of the gathering at Puivert, Bernart, according to the chronology generally accepted for his life, was in his late forties or early fifties, his principal amours probably behind him, and many of the poems relating to his liaisons no doubt were known by heart in that company, and also who the songs referred to. If he had really come from humble origins it would hardly have been worth Peire's devoting most of his stanza on Bernart to an elaborate sneer about his parentage. It would have been more in keeping with the kind of fun he was poking at all the guests if his allusion was to the legendary erotic activities of friends or relatives within the viscount's own circle, who indeed had been anything but humble. There are those who cherish the possibility that the ready bowman, in fact, was the viscount's own lord Guilhem IX, Comte de Peitau. It certainly would not have been foreign to what we know of his character and reputation.

As for Bernart's mother, the erotic implications of her heating the oven would have been unmistakable to everyone, and the bundling up of the vine shoots is not hard to interpret in the same vein. The suggestion would then be that Bernart's father was a well-known ladies' man in the Ventadorn circle, and that his mother's attractions and temperament were famous. If Bernart had been an indulged love child whom everyone in the extended family of the château had been pleased to watch growing up to be handsome and intelligent, it would explain, as the vida does not, how he came so easily to be literate, and more than ordinarily literate, and discovered early that he had a talent for composing poems in a highly cultivated convention, and singing them. Such circumstances would indicate that his name, Bernart de Ventadorn, was a family name and not merely a reference to his birthplace.

CHAPTER SEVEN

Then there are the poems. There is no way to tell what they may have included in his lifetime, but nearly fifty of them—twenty with their music—have survived, and from them we can reach tentative conclusions about him. These are not the few known accomplishments of cultivated members of the Limousin nobility in the twelfth or thirteenth century, like the literary remains of some of Bernart's neighbors, including some of the "four from Ussel" and Maria de Ventadorn. The poems of Bernart's that have come down to us comprise a consistent body of work with an authority and homogeneity of tone and language, a lyric artistry and assurance that, within the highly conventional mode that he was using, amount to a signature. All of his poems are love poems. In the latter part of the twelfth century, the high days of chivalry and of courtly love with its elaborately choreographed ambiguities, his poetry, in the estimation of many in his time and since, is the great articulation of his theme, in the forms of his age.

The two principal strains of troubadour poetry, once its tradition was established, were the *trobar leu*—the plain, or open style—and the hermetic, deliberately intricate *trobar clu*. Bernart was one of the great exemplars of the former, and though the conventions in which he wrote did not encourage the expression of private experience but the invention of stylized situations involving an unidentified beloved, a lyric purity and projection of feeling rings through his songs, and from the beginning must have made them memorable.

The poems are not all addressed to the same woman, but to several in a sequence that now cannot be determined. The Viscountess of Ventadorn and Aliénor of Aquitaine may have been his protectors, or something more intimate. Some passages in the poems are highly suggestive, but we are left only with that. The references to places known and longed for, and to journeys, speak of an unsettled life. His reference in a poem to the "school of Eble" is the source of the general belief that most of what he learned about poetry, about composing it, singing it, the sources of it, was probably acquired at Ventadorn, inside the château walls, where his principal mentor would no doubt have been Eble II, and where many of the troubadours of the first generations of the tradition may have come on visits at one time or another.

All that survived of Eble the Singer's own poetry was the reputation that clung to and became part of his name, and Bernart's tantalizing phrase. Yet it is possible to guess something of what must have been cultivated in that "school." The viscount was a friend and vassal of Guilhem IX, Comte de Peitau and Duke of Aquitaine, born about 1070, ten years after the first walls (parts of which can still be seen, where later dressed facings have fallen or have been broken away) were built at Ventadorn. Guilhem was powerful in every respect: a big man, decisive and full of energy, who at the age of fifteen had inherited domains larger and richer than the territory of his titular lord, the king of France, to whom he accorded a grudging allegiance. Headstrong, impatient, self-assured, one of the dominant political figures of Europe, Guilhem was made, and he behaved, in a grand manner. He loved the world, the life of the senses, love affairs, the arts of poetry and music, horses. His relations with the church, with the long fingers of Rome and the life-denying self-righteousness emanating from Bernard de Clairvaux, were abrasive. He was temporarily excommunicated for his interference with the ecclesiastical power structure. When he died in 1126 or 1127, he was buried in the Abbey of Montierneuf, which he had dedicated, but nothing there now marks his grave.

The news of Guilhem's death would have reached Ventadorn (according to the chronology most scholars have agreed on) when Bernart was a boy, and to Eble II it may have represented a great loss, for Guilhem was not only his lord and friend (even though the two were said to have been rivals in certain respects) but a poet of renowned talent and originality, who had brought to the composition of his songs the same passion and style that he directed toward everything else. He had been one of the most gifted poets of his generation in Europe. He had written in Occitan, and poems of his—ten, perhaps eleven of them, and music for at least one—would be the first ones in the language, and in the troubadour tradition, to survive.

Geoffrey de Vigeois, an early chronicler of the period, relates an anecdote about Guilhem and his vassal Eble the Singer that may be wholly apocryphal but gives some notion of the legends that came to circulate around them.

Eble, he says, who was the brother of Pierre-Buffière, gave great pleasure to Guilhem, the Count of Poitiers, with his skill in singing. There was a rivalry between the two men, each of them watching the other carefully to try to find the slightest sign of lack of courtesy which might detract from the other's renown. One day Eble arrived at Poitiers at the hour when his lord was at table. They served him a sumptuous dinner, but the preparations for it took a long time. When the meal was over, Eble said to the count, "Really, there was no need to go to such expense to entertain a mere viscount like me."

Shortly after that, when Eble had gone home again, Guilhem arrived almost upon his heels, exactly at the hour when Eble dined, and rushed in at the gate with over a hundred knights.

It was obvious to Eble that the count wanted to play a trick on him in his own way, and he had water poured for them to wash their hands, and while they were doing that he sent for food to all the villagers in the neighborhood, and it was brought in to the kitchen as quickly as could be. There was a great pile of chickens, ducks, all kind of fowl. In a little while they served up a feast fit for a king's wedding.

When the daylight was beginning to go, without a word having been said to Eble about it, a man from the village came in with a wagon behind him drawn by a pair of oxen, and he called out, "Come here, knights of the Count of Poitiers, and see how we deliver wax to the court of my lord the Viscount." Then he climbed onto the cart with a big carpenter's ax, and split open the barrels there, and out poured great quantities of candles of the finest wax. The peasant turned around as though what he had brought was of no importance at all, and went back to the village of Maumont.

Guilhem, after this, never tired of praising the nobility and courtesy of his vassal.

Later, Eble rewarded the peasant by giving him and his descendants the fief of Maumont. In due course they were knighted, and today they are the nephews of Archambaud of Solignac, and of Alboenus, the archdeacon of Limoges.

If it ever happened at all, it happened here. But it sounds like a tale, a bit of pure invention, that had once been locally familiar, and must have been improved by many retellings. Not so much a popular story, perhaps, as a bit of court gossip developing as it was being retold, toward the *Gesta Romanorum* and the surprises of fairy tales. It is less concerned with what happened or might have happened than with exemplifying a manner, an attitude, an image of the way the ruling class, the nobility, liked to think of themselves in the great courts from Poitiers to Blaye, Toulouse, and the Pyrénées. The word that has come to us from that time and setting to describe it would be largesse.

Among other things, the story presents a contemporary view of the nature of nobility. In Eble II's domain at Ventadorn, this high, unhesitating, uncalculating liberality is portrayed as a distinction of Eble's own character and as something that has permeated his entire domain, even to the peasants in the nearby villages, so that the peasant who brings the wagonload of candles and then leaves as though they were nothing displays noble liberality—or what they referred to as courtesy—in the high manner, and was rewarded appropriately.

In Guilhem's realm, and no doubt in Eble II's court, the code derived in part from a current of arts and manners, habits of taste, pleasure, and admiration that had been traveling north in waves from Arabic Spain, and included not only poetry and song and music, but highly involved conventions relating to behavior, and to the forms, subjects, situations, and attitudes proper to poetry.

Guilhem, in his best years, must have been an immensely impressive figure, whose tastes and magnetism encouraged emulation among the nobility, from Poitiers southward. He represented power on a regal scale, and the unpredictable authority of a lively headlong temperament, like that of a great conductor or theatrical director.

Minstrels, jongleurs, had traveled from court to court before Guilhem's day. They seldom composed the songs they sang, in which the music came first, and the words were fitted to it. The wandering life had allowed the minstrels to pick up strains of melody and verses from widely scattered areas. We do not know exactly what kinds of music and lyrics Guilhem grew up hearing, but in the eleventh century the ruling class in the Poitou and the Limousin probably associated pleasure with the south, the lands of the Romanized Celtic people of the Aquitaine, and the Christian and Arabic kingdoms on the far side of the Pyrénées. Guilhem had been considered an indolent child, and when his father died suddenly, apparently on a hunting party, he was still referred to as a boy. He inherited his father's love of traveling, fighting, politics, women, and also the high spirits and taste for entertainment of his gentle, Burgundian mother. He had a tutor who taught him a certain amount of Latin, including, apparently, some of the poetry of Ovid. He must have had a music teacher. The influence of Ovid on Spanish-Arabic poets in the early eleventh century found its way north, and eventually became part of the code of chivalry and of courtly love and the poetry that went with them, of which Viscount Eble's court would become one of the great nurseries.

Guilhem's first marriage ended quickly in divorce. His second wife, whom he married in 1094, when he was twenty-three, was Spanish. She was Philippa, the twenty-two-year-old widow of King Sancho of Aragón, and she brought with her to Poitiers Andalusian singers and composers of lyrics who had been influenced by Arabic music and song. Probably she brought Arabic musicians and dancers with her too.

It was only a few months later that Pope Urban II, at Clermont, in the Auvergne, began to drum up the First Crusade. He and his clerical entourage arrived to visit the newly married Guilhem and Philippa, and stayed to preach the holy war under the ducal auspices for twenty-five days. Eventually, in March 1101 (seven years after the pope had started his incitements), Guilhem reluctantly led an army, supplied by William the Red of England, from Poitiers toward the east. There were some 160,000 of them when they reached Constantinople, where the army merged with other units and grew to nearly double that number. The entire expedition set off across Asia Minor and was ambushed, surrounded, and scattered in the dry mountains. Thousands were killed, many thousands more died in the desert.

Many—the women in particular—were hauled off into slavery. Guilhem escaped to Antioch, and made his way back to Poitiers at the end of 1102.

He had spent most of a year in Antioch and Palestine as a guest of Tancred, the commander there. The bitterness of the defeat and of the vast losses, which were said to be the fault of their guide, Raymond de Saint-Gilles, must have weighed heavily upon him, and no doubt Tancred did his best to entertain him. Antioch at that time was one of the great commercial and cultural centers of the world. Its wealth and eminence had grown with each of the successive civilizations—Greek, Roman, Persian, Byzantine—that had formed its history. Generation after generation the arts had flowered there, or had been brought there along the caravan routes, and north and south trade routes through Asia Minor, and from across the Mediterranean. It was a magnificent city, with a deep, intricate, many-layered splendor, in a setting of great natural beauty. And there no doubt Guilhem heard Arabic and Asian music and poetry as a frequent accompaniment to his days, and the memories of it, and perhaps songs and singers from Antioch, traveled back with him to Poitiers, where they must have been welcome reminders of the sumptuous eastern city.

His own later poetry (if we have its order correctly), after the crushing failure of the campaign, and the court life of Antioch, is more distinctive than his earlier pieces. Its variety is greater, almost certainly as a result of what he had heard and remembered. The six or seven years after his return from the Crusade—1102-1108—may have been the high plateau in his life, when his own court flourished and was most admired, and when the arts and what would come to be the mannered code of courtly love took form there.

But regional divisions in the structure of his domain and lack of money (which the Crusade had also lost in huge quantities) became insoluble problems ten years after he came back to Poitiers. He taxed church property and was excommunicated for it by the bishop of Poitiers, whom he put into prison, where the bishop died. One of his amours proved to be particularly ill-advised. He fell in love with the wife of Aimeri I of Châtellerault, a woman with the unequivocal name of Dangereuse, and the papal legate, after chiding him for the affair, which had become a widespread embarrassment, confirmed the bishop of Poitiers' excommunication. As a result of the scandal, Guilhem's wife retired to the Abbey of Fontevrault the same year that the bishop died, and she herself died three years later.

Guilhem finally came to terms with the pope, and the excommunication was lifted, but his entire disparate domain had become a fabric of factions and dissensions. In 1120, the year in which Bernart may have been born, Guilhem led a force of six hundred knights to the aid of the King of Aragón, in what may have been an effort to patch up his relations with that family and repair his own reputation. The combined forces won an important victory over the Almoravids at Cutanda, and on the way home Guilhem resolved his difficulties with the counts of Toulouse. But troubles or the threat of troubles continued to widen crevices in his territories for the rest of his life.

Yet the great years of his court, the magnet it had become for the arts and for the nascent attitudes of chivalry, had initiated in a few years a current of poetry and a pattern of tastes and attitudes that would reach maturity during the next two generations, and even after the apocalypse of the Albigensian Crusade would go on to influence and color the whole subsequent culture of Europe and the Western world.

His poems must have served as primal models in the sudden proliferation of lyrics that circulated in the courts of Languedoc soon after his were written. Though he is generally credited with being the first of the troubadours because his poems are the earliest ones that have survived, there is no way of knowing whether he was the only poet writing in Occitan when he began. It is evident that his lyrics drew together several currents of verse and ideas, and probably of music, and it is hard not to believe that there were song lyrics before his in Occitan, perhaps set to melodies picked up or adapted from Spanish-Arabic singers visiting the Aquitainian courts, their verses following the formal patterns of Arabic poems that had suggested them, and their diction introducing an element imported into European poetry from Arabic: rhyme. Of course Guilhem would also have known popular songs, folk songs, in Poitevin, Occitan, Catalan, and other Romance languages, from his childhood onward. In 1064, seven years before Guilhem was born, his father had led an army into Spain to join his friend and ally King Sancho of Aragón, and together they had besieged and taken the rich Arabic citadel of Barbastro. Among the Poitevin spoils were several famous Moorish women singers, who presumably were taken back to Poitiers and installed at the court there, and their singing would have been some of the earliest that Guilhem would remember. When as a young man, he led his army to Spain to fight in alliance with King Sancho, and married Sancho's widow, he stayed there for months before returning north. He was typical of the fact that temperamentally, socially, culturally, politically, in the eleventh and twelfth centuries the nobility of the region of Languedoc had a clearer affinity with Spain than with France north of the Loire. It is no wonder that six of his surviving ten or eleven poems follow, in Occitan, the verse form of the Arabic *zajal*.

The few distant echoes of Ovid's *Art of Love* that have been identified in Guilhem's poems may also have come to him, and have passed on into the courts of love, from Arabic Spain. Ovid was circulated in western Europe in the eleventh century, in translation as well as in Latin. His profane, sensual, poetic treatise (which is said to have been a cause of his exile) was popular, and the views it presented may have been talked about even among those who had not actually read it. Guilhem was not a scholar but a man of action, probably not much of a reader, but he may have heard passages of Ovid read aloud while he was growing up. Fifty years before Guilhem was born, Ovid's poem, as well as Plato on the subject of love, were known to the Andalusian Arab writer Ibn Hazm, who wrote his own treatise on love, *The Dove's Neck-Ring*, combining elements of both of them, and Arabic sources as well—a work that profoundly influenced Spanish-Arabic poets in the centuries that followed, and through the troubadours and the courts of Languedoc, and eventually of Troyes and Blois, helped to shape the ideals of courtly love, unresolved between sensuality and sublimation, "true love" and common love. Guilhem's poems, his court, his character indicate a thoroughly sensual Ovidian view of the subject. But the court and "school" of his younger vassal and immediate successor in the encouragement of song and poetry, Eble II, may have been one of the leading places where more complex attitudes toward the subject were developed.

However the influences upon Guilhem came together, his best poems strike notes that still sound fresh and new, and there is a tone that remains his own even as it echoes in the words of later poets for generations. No other early poem that I know carries the cast of feeling suggested and dramatized in *Ab la dolchor del temps novel,* which begins with the season that would become emblematic of all the love poetry of the troubadours, and of the great period of their poetry as a whole: spring. The month of May. Without music, and with the inevitable removes of translation, it goes like this:

> With the sweetness of the new season
> woods fill with leaves and the birds sing
> each of them in its own tongue *(en lor lati)*
> set to the verse of a new song,
> then is the time a man should bring
> himself to where his heart has gone.
>
> From my best and fairest to me
> no messenger nor seal I see
> so my heart neither laughs nor sleeps
> nor do I dare take further steps
> until I know that we agree
> it is as I want it to be.

The way this love of ours goes on
is like the branch of the hawthorn
that keeps trembling upon the tree
in the night in the rain and ice
until the sun comes and the day
spreads through the green leaves and branches.

I can still recall one morning
when we put an end to warring
and how great was the gift she then
gave me: her love and her ring.
God, just let me live to getting
my hand under her cloak again!

What do I care for the strange way
they talk to keep my love away?
I know how words are, how they go
everywhere, one hint is enough.
They talk of love, what do they know?
We have the morsel and the knife.

In view of what would happen to the troubadour tradition—
the intimidation brought on by the church and by the crusading
horrors that heralded the Inquisition, and the abstraction and
sublimation of the erotic urge, and the stylized idealization cul-
minating in the otherworldly projection of Dante's eternal
Beatrice—it is a relief to know that the tradition began with a
passion that was unquestionably mortal and physical. This poem
of Guilhem's and its tone remind me, above all in the fourth

stanza, of a poet and man of action more than four centuries later, who can be thought of as a remote poetic heir, Sir Thomas Wyatt.

And here, in one of the first love poems of the troubadours, is the hawthorn, known too in English as the mayflower, the may: the wild, white (or occasionally pink or red) flower opening in clusters or corymbs, with an almondy fragrance not altogether sweet, and needle-sharp thorns, that came to symbolize in the troubadour tradition the season of love and the hope of its return, of seeing it again.

The rose came later, in the poetry and in the season. Weeks after the moment Guilhem described, in which drifts of minute hawthorn petals glittered in the still freezing nights, some of the mays would still be in flower as the first eglantines opened their single corollas, which seldom lasted for more than a day. And for Guilhem's vassal, Jaufre Rudel, the flowering hawthorn represented the end of winter, while the first eglantines opening, and the song of the nightingales (they begin to sing in Aquitaine in the last days of April) announced the coming of spring.

Cultivated varieties of certain rose species had been grown in Persia and in Roman gardens—ancestors, perhaps, of the Portlands, Damasks, and Gallicas. Some may have been cared for in monastery gardens, and it is known that some were brought back, with difficulty that we can scarcely imagine, from the Crusades, and they took their places in the imagination, the symbols and legends and cathedral windows of Europe. But first there was the hawthorn, and it was wild. Guilhem's likening his (no doubt reckless and undomesticated) love to the modest, dauntless hawthorn flower comes to us like a testament of authenticity.

His choice of flower to represent his passion, and his love of words (without which he would never have composed his lyrics) were shared, nearer to our own time, by Marcel Proust. Centuries later, Proust wrote of walking, as a child, with his parents on the footpath that he associated with the little girl he was in love with, and finding the whole lane "throbbing with the fragrance of hawthorn blossom." In a later time and from a vastly different temperament, he discoursed upon the hawthorn and then upon the emotion it represented, with a detailed opulence far removed from Guilhem's spare image, complete and suggestive as a cave painting.

To Proust, as he remembered it, the hedge resembled a series of chapels, their walls hidden by mountains of flowers heaped on the altars. The scent, that elusive guide of memory, lured him even more insistently than the sight itself. "But it was in vain," he wrote, "that I lingered before the hawthorns, to breathe in, to marshal before my mind (which knew not what to make of it), *to lose in order to rediscover* their invisible and unchanging odour...but in vain did I shape my fingers into a frame, so as to have nothing but the hawthorns before my eyes; the sentiment which they aroused in me remained obscure and vague, struggling and failing to free itself, to float across and become one with the flowers. They themselves offered me no enlightenment, and I could not call upon any other flowers to satisfy this mysterious longing."

I have italicized the words *to lose in order to rediscover* because they summarize a perspective that has come to be thought of as characteristically Proustian and hence "modern," but which in fact can be found in the romantic tradition as far back as we can identify its origins. Proust's passion is the early, as yet unnamed erotic longing of childhood. He was spellbound by the hawthorns (or so he remembers it) just before he learned that the name of the little girl with whom he had fallen in love at first sight was Gilberte. Guilhem's is the focused desire of a grown man, determined, in full awareness of the hostility of circumstances, and the obstacles to his desire. But for both of them the hawthorn, the may, represents their feeling.

Guilhem's clear, immediate poem, its unabashed sensual hunger, its season, its hawthorn in flower, passed into the poetry that would come after him, which he would never know anything about. His lyrics and those of the later troubadours were not (in their time) simply read. They were sung over and over, and were known by heart, not only by their singers but by many in their audiences, as popular songs are in every age. This lyric about the hawthorn, both its words and its music, would have been familiar to everyone at Ventadorn—probably not only to the gentry in their halls and chambers but also to the retainers coming and going in the castle—and Bernart, if he was the age that seems probable, would have grown up hearing it. There are recurrences of its feeling, its tone, and adaptations of Arabic verse forms such as Guilhem had made, and again the hawthorn, in Bernart's own lyrics.

Guilhem's invocation of the hawthorn flower to represent something so personal, so intimate and spontaneous as the love between him and his beloved, was in fact already deeply rooted in tradition. In the Occitan region the arrival of the month of May as the returning season of love had been celebrated with festivals since long before Christianity. The rites of spring were remnants of fertility ceremonies practiced in the time of the Roman occupation and among the Celtic peoples long before that. The name of the month, and of the mayflower in English, is thought to be a derivation of Maja or Maia, the earth goddess in many religions, and from Magja, the ancient one, the earth, in Sanskrit, and from Megha in Indo-European, meaning "great."

Festivals in honor of the spring were held all through the Aquitaine and in Spain as far south as Andalusia. On the first of May women and girls made decorations of hawthorn flowers to celebrate the arrival of the month, during which young men wore a "cap of youth" and love was indulged, we are assured, without the restrictions and obligations that held it in check throughout the rest of the year. Women, even married women, enjoyed, it is said, their old freedom. They elected a queen representing the season for them, and the young men elected a "chief of youth" who alone had the right to wear hawthorn flowers at the festivals, and the flowers may have symbolized other privileges. The festivities, and perhaps some of the privileges, continued in parts of those regions up until the First World War. (The word *mayur*, of all things, appears to have been derived from the ancient meanings during the late Middle Ages.) Hawthorn flowers were long used in love potions. As late as the nineteenth century, peasants in the Languedoc did not exchange marriage vows or hold weddings in the month of May.

Another poem of Guilhem's, not a love lyric, continued to reverberate in the songs of the troubadours who followed him. *Farai un vers de dreit rien,* one of his most enigmatic poems, seems to dismiss any curiosity about what may have suggested it. The sense of it is:

I'll make a song of pure nothing,
not about me or another being,
not about love or being young
or anything.
It came to me while I was sleeping
on my horse riding.

The hour I was born is unknown to me.
I am not happy nor unhappy,
neither aloof nor friendly,
and the choice is not mine:
I am what a fairy made me
at night on a mountain.

I cannot say whether I
am asleep or awake. Somebody tell me.
My heart is nearly broken by
a pain I feel
for which I will not even sigh,
by St. Martial.

I'm sick and fear that I will die
and all I know of it is hearsay.
I want a doctor who pleases me
I don't know who.
He'll be good if he can cure me;
if it gets worse, no.

I have a lover I don't know.

Never saw her. No use to.
No good or ill to me did she do
that I could notice
nor ever was Norman or Frenchman who
was in my house.

I never saw her but love her warmly.
I was never right and she never wronged me.
When I don't see her I manage nicely,
don't give a rooster.
I know one with more charm and beauty,
and her better.

I've made the verse, whose is unknown,
and I'll give it to that one
who'll pass it on to someone
going toward Anjou
so she'll send back a countersign
in his portmanteau.

The dimension of existence that is beyond any reason or
expression or conception would seem, in itself, to pertain to a
kind of metaphysical subtlety with which Guilhem would have
had little patience. Yet he may have been acquainted with the
idea of inexpressible, intangible reality not only from hearing
contemporary discussions of mysticism and its tradition but
from Spanish-Arabic poetry, where it was a recurring subject.

His poem is echoed, a full generation later, in what is probably the greatest poem of Bernart's contemporary, Raimbaut

d'Aurenga, who was present, and may have been the guest of honor, at Peire d'Alvernhe's banquet at Puivert. He is the ninth poet in Peire's poem. Peire's satire pretends to chide Raimbaut for making his songs too beautiful, but Peire says, "I will bring them to nothing. They're neither hot nor cold, and worth no more than the pipes of those that go begging." He is alluding to the poem of Raimbaut's that begins *"Escotz, mas no say que s'es"* (Listen, but I don't know what it is), a composition that repeatedly reduces expectations to the unknown, apparent sense to its opposite, verse to refrains in prose, appearances to questions that remain unanswerable. "Lady," he says at the end of one stanza, "you can do as you like with it, as Ayma did with the shoulder bone, sticking it where she pleased."

Some scholars have believed that Raimbaut was the "Tristan" to whom Bernart addressed his own great poem, perhaps one of his last, which begins with the lark's wing and ends with his own sense of being reduced to nothing. The end of that poem may also be an heir of Guilhem's strange song of nothing, which of course Bernart would have known all his life.

CHAPTER EIGHT

In the generation that followed Guilhem's, many of the early
troubadours, including neighbors from Ussel, some of the other
poets who would be named in Peire d'Alvernhe's satire, others
who left a few poems or whose work vanished without a trace,
must have stayed at Ventadorn while Bernart was growing up
there. Jongleurs, musicians, rehearsals, new songs, performances in the great hall—some of the châteaus in the region had
minstrel galleries built in the dining halls, like choir lofts in
churches. Discussion of the lyrics and the music, all may have
been part of his days there, along with the countryside and
arms, and horses.

Appel devoted years of study trying to deduce from internal
evidence in Bernart's surviving poems some sequence that would
allow him to discern an outline of Bernart's life. The conventions
of troubadour poetry were not designed for confessional revelations,

but Appel's delicate reconstruction may bring us as close as we will ever be to the main elements of his story.

The recurring burden of Bernart's song is distance—a constant theme of the love poetry of the world—the distance between the lover and the beloved, between the present and the past or an imagined future, between one place and another, social difference, difference of temperament and character. The tenor of the word *longing* itself is part of that, and *amor de lonh* (far away love) became essential to the tradition of the troubadours. Distance is a measure of absence. Even in Guilhem's love poem with its candid sensuality, the beloved is out of reach, too far to hear him, there is no message from her, he remembers another time when they were together.

The reaching out to her absence is another gesture linking his song with the poetry of Arabic Spain. As early as the ninth century, even before the great treatises on love were written on the Iberian Peninsula, a poet named Sa'id Ibn Sulaiman Ibn Gudi addressed three poems to a slave girl with whom he had fallen helplessly in love without ever having seen her, upon hearing her singing to the emir.

Early in the eleventh century, when Ibn Hazm, the great Spanish-Arabic philosopher-poet, a man of immense culture and erudition, who had been brought up in the utmost luxury, surrounded by the arts and taught by highly educated women, wrote his treatise on love, *The Dove's Neck-Ring,* it soon became a textbook for generations of Arab poets.

His work is divided into thirty chapters dealing with what he considered to be every aspect of love, including the classical dramatis personae of a love story—the messenger, the helping friend, the fault-finder, the slanderer, the watcher—and the developments to be expected, such as betrayal, avoidance, rupture, oblivion. Of separation he says, "There is no misfortune in the world that equals separation, and there are various kinds of it," and he proceeds to list and describe them.

He enumerates various ways of falling in love. In the chapter on "Love At First Sight," he tells of the poet Yusuf ibn Harun, known as Al-Ramadi, passing by the Gate of the Perfumers in Cordova, which was a gathering place for women, and seeing there a young *gariya,* a slave girl, who took possession of all his heart, and love for her penetrated into all the members of his body. He followed her as she went up toward the bridge. She crossed it to a place known as Al-Rabad, and when she was passing among the tombstones of Banu Marwan on the other side of the river, she looked at him, separated as he was from all the others, and intent upon nothing but her, and she went toward him and said, "Why are you walking behind me?" And he told her of the great agitation he felt because of her. She said, "Cast this away from you, and do not try to shame me, for there is no use expecting the fulfillment of your intention, and no way to obtain what you desire." He said then, "I shall be content with looking at you." And she said, "You are allowed to do that." He asked her, "My lady, are you free or a slave?" She said, "A slave." He asked her, "What is your name?" She said "Halwa" (Solitude). He said, "To whom do you belong?" She answered, "Your knowledge of what is in the seventh heaven is nearer to you than what you have asked about, so stop your foolish talk." And he said to her, "My lady, when shall I see you after this?" She said, "Where you saw me today, about the same hour, on

Friday." Then she asked, "Will you go away first, or shall I?" He said, "You go first, with God's protection." She started toward the bridge and he could not go after her, because she was watching to see whether he was following her. "By God," he said, "I went assiduously to the Perfumers' Gate and Al-Rabad from that time on, but never heard another thing about her. And I do not know whether the heavens consumed her or the earth swallowed her up, but truly there is in my heart, because of her, a burning fiercer than a glowing ember." And she was the Halwa to whom he addressed his love poems.

An Arab poet who followed Ibn Hazm, Ibn Zaidun, was in love with a cultivated, autocratic, daring, red-haired princess, herself a poet, named Wallada, who was the center of a group of poets. She never allowed Ibn Zaidun to be sure of her, but she resented any attention that she thought he might be paying to anyone else—her black maid, for instance. The tone and circumstances of the complaints in his poems must also have been familiar to the troubadours, and influenced the manner in which they wrote of their own amours.

And although many of the Arabic erotic poems seem to have been written about flesh-and-blood passions and addressed to living people, the motif of the beloved seen once and then loved obsessively for the rest of a lifetime became a convention. Among the troubadours, Guilhem's vassal, Jaufre Rudel, of the generation between Guilhem and Bernart, addressed his songs to a distant love. The legend that was built up out of the amor de lonh in his poems, which became fixed in his *vida,* tells how he fell in love with the countess of Tripoli without ever having seen her, simply from what he had heard about her from pilgrims coming back from Antioch, and how, having written many songs about her, he was driven by a desire to see her, and became a crusader and took ship, but fell sick on the voyage and was dying when the vessel reached Tripoli and he was carried to an inn. The countess learned about him, came to his bedside, and he died in her arms. The actual facts of Jaufre Rudel's life are if anything even more uncertain than those of Bernart's. He may have visited Ventadorn in Bernart's youth, and surely his songs would have been familiar there.

More than a century after Jaufre Rudel, an Italian poet who certainly knew his poems, Dante's friend Guido Cavalcanti, caught sight of Mandetta only once, in a church in Toulouse, and addressed his love poems to her for the rest of his life. And then of course there are Dante's Beatrice and Petrarch's Laura, with regard to whom distance had been extended into death and transfiguration. By that time it was not uncommon in Western philosophy for the explication of something to take the form of demonstrating that it represented something else, and the idealization of women and sublimation of the erotic urge had been transmuted into a spiritual quest, the secret goal of a great fairy tale. After all that, I am glad to think that an Arab slave girl, indeed the overheard song of an Arab slave girl, may have been the true ancestor of the exalted Beatrice.

Even the use of the *senhal,* the fictitious name of the person to whom the troubadour's poems were addressed—and the source, inevitably, of endless biographical speculation—may have been adapted from Spanish-Arabic ancestors. It became part of a code in Bernart's poems that Appel labored to decipher. There, some of the names appear to signify lovers, others perhaps patrons, friends, other troubadours. Were they ever real secrets, or merely masks on sticks at a costume dance? Or was their actual function something that varied with the circumstances and the passage of time? When the poems referred to the phases of actual love affairs the need for secrecy or disguise is easy to imagine, especially as there must have been little privacy within castle walls. (It was cold and dark there, besides, for months on end, and it is hard to imagine the inhabitants being eager to take off all their clothes, or indeed to wash as often as might have been nice. No wonder spring was thought of as the time for love, and May Day outings were intent on more things than wild flowers.) In any event, the senhals of Bernart's poems are not always concealing the same thing, and some of the poems exist in several versions each with a different senhal.

After all his painstaking hypothetical reconstructions Appel concluded that we can be certain of two things about Bernart: He was born and grew up at Ventadorn, and he had a close relation of some kind, for a number of years, with Aliénor of Aquitaine, both before she married Henry II of England, and then later, for a year or so, at the English court. Proponents of the possibility that Bernart was an illegitimate son of Count Guilhem IX's later amours point to the apparent ease of Bernart's attachment to Aliénor—who according to that theory would have been his own kin—and to its survival through her own changing circumstances. But for all its attractions, there is no more evidence for or against this hypothesis than there is with the others.

Many of Bernart's earlier poems may have been written at Ventadorn before he left there, or upon returns after journeys, and it seems likely that he had at least one long attachment to a love there, of whom he wrote:

> ever since we were
> both children I have loved her

She may or may not be the same one about whom, in another poem, he says:

> Ventadorn will not lack for a singer
> since she who is noblest and knows most
> about love taught me all I know

and she may also be the one of whom he sings:

> I am lost to my friends at Ventadorn
> now my lady no longer loves me;
> I do well not to go there again,
> her way with me is so rude and sullen.

Whether that one, or any of them, was the viscountess, no one knows.

Appel believed that Aliénor's patronage, friendship, or whatever it was, took Bernart to England, but that there, for whatever reason, he stopped composing songs, a silence that lasted for two years. When he wrote again, if Appel got the order of his poems right, the favors of the lady he tells of had receded into the past. She dismisses his suit as though there had never been anything between them. He is in England, across the wild sea, with winter coming, and he hopes to see his beloved before winter arrives—if it please the king. But

> She sends word to me
> that fear prevents her
> from doing more for me.

That one, we can assume, was Aliénor, and if so, she had good reason for anxiety. Henry Plantagenet embodied volatile energy combined with a raw crudeness and ruthlessness that recurred in his behavior and in that of several of his descendants including his son John—King John of the Magna Carta. Some years after Bernart had left England, and a few months after Peire d'Alvernhe's banquet at Puivert in 1173, when Aliénor had separated from Henry and had set up her own domain, with its famous court of love, in her grandfather Guilhem's city of Poitiers, Henry's army devastated castles and countryside from Tours to Poitiers, burning, destroying villages, fortresses, orchards, and vineyards, slaughtering, and hauling off prisoners to the dungeons of Normandy. They sent hunting parties searching for Aliénor, but failed to find her until Henry's scouts saw a small group of knights fleeing through the smoking wasteland north of Poitiers, ran them down, and found among them Aliénor, dressed as a knight, surrounded by a ragged remnant of her entourage. Henry took Aliénor and her escort prisoner, transported them to England, and locked them all up, Aliénor herself in Salisbury Tower, and she did not regain her freedom

for six years. Among her retainers at the last were several troubadours who had been in attendance at her court. Years earlier,
in England, if she spoke to Bernart about her need for caution,
she must have had no illusions about the character of the king
who was her second husband.

In another song, written apparently in the spring, after his
dreaded winter, Bernart says she has given him reason to be
hopeful, yet the separation between them continues. The vicis-
situdes of Aliénor's fortunes and of his, over a period of several
years, are beyond tracing at all, but some time later Bernart
appears to have traveled from England to a chivalric gathering
at the court of Puy, nearer home, and he wrote songs for the
occasion. Their theme, as that of most of his poems of those
years, was separation from the one he loved. Which could be,
and perhaps was meant to be, construed in several ways. Some
poems, or parts of some poems, may refer to a patron or protector, others to a lover—and perhaps even to the one he had loved
for so long at Ventadorn, but the code finally keeps its secrets.

Other songs of Bernart's that seem to have been written in
the following years indicate journeys, benefactors, the travails
of love and separation. Some were written in the Auvergne, and
in the region south of Lyon around Vienne, and in Toulouse. It
is possible that the real beloved is the same person in, or
behind, all or most of them, with the dedications and stanzas
alluding to circumstances of his life, varying with the occasions.
There must have been benefactors after Aliénor. Among those
who have been suggested are Constance, the wife of Count
Raimon of Toulouse, Richildis, the widow of Count Raimon
Berenger II of Provence, the Countess of Vienne, Marguerite de

Bourgogne, and Ermengarde, Viscountess of Narbonne, a patron of many troubadours.

If Bernart finally settled, as the vida tells us, at the court of Count Raimon V of Toulouse, we know that the count his patron died in 1194, when Bernart, according to most calculations, was seventy or more. But that too is speculation. Moshe Lazar, a French scholar who published an edition of Bernart's poems in 1966, half a century after Appel's, wrote that "we should humbly confess our total ignorance of the life of Bernart de Ventadorn, his origins, his destiny, and his end."

CHAPTER NINE

Dante, whose familiarity with the Occitan language of his own and the troubadours' time no one now could match, considered Arnaut Daniel the greatest of those poets. Dante's judgments, by the time he was writing the later parts of the *Commedia* especially, were sometimes schematically influenced in ways that reflect his own moment and situation. He had reason to be anxious about the figure he cut in the eyes of the church, and that concern may have influenced him in placing Folquet de Marseilla—another troubadour, and a slippery, self righteous, cruel opportunist, a shameful example of any tradition—prominently in his Paradise, along with Domingo de Guzmán, the father of the Inquisition, whom the church canonized as Saint Dominic. Both of them may be there, at least partly, because of their roles in the sectarian cleansing of the Cathar "heretics" who had been so outrageous as to choose what they believed. Dante had good reasons for wanting to set himself as far as possible from anything that might be construed as sympathy with heresies.

His unequaled admiration for Arnaut Daniel seems to have been based on the consummate skill with which Daniel handled the formal and linguistic intricacies of the *trobar clu,* the closed style. But in fact, the way Dante speaks of himself and his art in Canto XXIV of the *Purgatorio:*

> I am one who, when
> Love breathes in me, take note, and as it is
> dictated within, go setting it down

sounds closer to Bernart's practice than to Daniel's, and Bernart, like Dante, wrote on the theme of love all his life. One of Bernart's poems begins by stating it as a principle:

> No use singing, it seems to me,
> unless the song comes from the heart,
> and song cannot come from the heart
> unless true love is there already.

Dante was able to make the theme of love, syllogistically at least, include many forms of experience and vast reaches of human action and history. But even Bernart's great editor Appel, who cared deeply for Bernart's poetry, seems to have wished that his subject had been more varied, and he spoke of that limitation somewhat apologetically. Yet songwriters and singers, including some of the greatest, in every age since his, from Dante's Casella to Edith Piaf and Billie Holiday, have sung only of love, and have not been considered disappointing because of that. Bernart seems to have understood the nature of his gift from the beginning, and to have remained true to it. The spoken usages of his words are almost entirely lost to us now, but even across these distances of time and language and culture it is still possible, with patience, to overhear in passage after passage of his lyrics the light play of meaning, the delicacy and authenticity of a great songwriter. His mastery is not based on a display of intricacy, as Arnaut Daniel's is. Bernart has been called the Racine of the troubadours, in reference, I suppose, to the limpidity of his lines and the beauty of his diction, but the comparison also suggests how much of the musical transparency of his poetry is likely to be lost in translation.

The tongue in which he wrote has suffered the damages not only of time but of deliberate disregard and neglect. Almost all that remains of it in its ancient form is the poetry. In our age it is an idiom not dead, but no longer spoken in the old way, archaic, like the English of Chaucer, and with no surviving original voice, no voice at all except what we bring to it. It is still possible to learn the sounds, more or less, and the grammar that relates them, but the native intonation, the common utterance, the second nature, is irretrievable. Even so, something of the ancient elegance of phrase, assonance, and musical grace can be heard by those who care to listen. There will not be many of them, but the hearing of poetry is something that happens to audiences of one, even when they are surrounded by others. All this is true of the poetry of the classical languages of the ancient world too, which are no longer spoken at all; and most ironically of all (because such survival depends entirely on what has been written down) it is true of the poetry of oral traditions in which the native use has ceased. What poetry may remain for us in any of them now is inseparable from the apparatus of reconstruction, including the attempts at translation. And with the troubadours, as with many of these other traditions, much of the music to which the words were wedded has been lost, and what survives also relies upon latter-day rehabilitation, after centuries filled with very different music and the associations around it. Even when we can manage to reproduce more or less what they heard, it is impossible to know how it sounded to them.

Standing in the ruins of what is now known as Ventadour, or pronouncing the words of Bernart's text, it is not only the syllables of the ancient *roman* tongue that we want to hear, but the living flow of the whole poetry, and the best we can catch is halting, broken, and foreign. But the craving to hear it is what brings us back to all poetry, of our own time or any other, hoping that something has been carried across a great distance like water in the hands: the life of the original. Translations try again and again to convey its clear note and are left hearkening past themselves toward the elusive source. Sometimes we can hear Bernart most distinctly in fragments:

> Let someone sing who wants to sing;
> I do not know the way there now
> since I lost what made me happy.
>
> *
>
> All the joy in the world is ours,
> lady, if we love each other
>
> *

Oh what is my life to me
unless every day I see
my own true joy
in bed or from the window

*

Let her be daring enough
one night to take all her clothes off
and conduct me to a good place
with my neck in her embrace.

*

With joy I begin the verse
and with joy bring it to a close.

*

Lady, my heart,
the best friend I have,
I send you as a hostage
until I come back from here.

Besides the theme of separation, and the expression of suffering, both real and dramatized, we can hear from a later age
altogether, through all the songs, the troubadour love poets'
assumption of eternal youth.

Most of the poems of Bernart's that have survived were
doubtless well known in his lifetime and in the years that followed, during and after the massacres of the Albigensian Crusade
that so altered the tone of the century that followed them. One of
Bernart's lyrics that often represents him may have been among
his last. Appel was of that opinion, and the poem's deep sadness
and note of summation and farewell make it seem likely. It is one

of those for which the music survives, and it can be heard now in several haunting recordings. It must have been sung at Ventadorn, but probably a long time after he had left the castle and the view down the valley and across the ridges, and the sound of the streams. The lark is not a bird of the woodlands but of open country. He sings at a great height, usually too high to see, and then, Bernart says, forgets himself and lets himself fall.

Quan Vei L'Alauzeta Mover

When I see how the lark beats
his wings in joy at the sun's ray
when he forgets himself and lets
himself fall with sweetness of heart
oh I feel such envy for
anyone I see in joy
it is a wonder that my heart
does not melt with its desire.

Alas, I knew so much, I thought,
about love, and I knew so little!
For there is no way for me not
to love her who yields none at all.
She took herself and took my heart,
my self and all the world with her,
went and left only desire
and the longing of my heart.

The ladies bring me to despair,

I will not trust them any more.
Long I argued in their favor
but I will not any longer
for none is any use to me
with her who wastes and ruins me.
I have lost faith in all of them
knowing that they are all the same.

Love is lost, that much is certain,
and I never even knew it.
The one in whom it should have been
has none. Where can I look for it?
Oh it looks harsh to those who see her
let this poor creature pine for her
who finds no good except in her,
and die, since no help comes from her.

Since God is no help with my lady
nor mercy, nor what she should give me,
and since it is not her pleasure
to love me, I will never tell her,
and if she rejects and shuns me,
she kills me, and from death I answer.
I will leave, unless she keeps me,
exiled, despairing, who knows where.

I have no will of my own,
nor have been my own since she
let me look into her eyes,

into that mirror that enchants me.
Since in you, mirror, I have seen
myself I perish with deep sighs.
I lost myself there the same way
as fair Narcissus in the fountain.

In this my lady seems like all
the rest, and I blame her for that.
She does not want what she ought to,
and she does what she should not do.
I have crossed the bridge like a fool
and fallen into her ill will.
How it happened I cannot say
unless perhaps I climbed too high.

Tristan, you'll hear no more from me,
I leave and cannot say for where,
sad at heart, and will sing no more
but hide myself from love and joy.

The sadness is there in the music too.

The other poet whose name and poetry are associated with
the château is Maria de Ventadorn, who lived there two generations after Bernart, around the end of the twelfth century. All
that survives of her poetry is half (the alternate stanzas) of
one *tenso*—a poetic exchange, with Gui d'Ussel, in which she
upholds with grace, eloquence, and authority the independence,
and the determining role of women in matters of love.

She is a brilliant example of the *trobairitz,* the women troubadours of her time. She was born Maria de Turena, one of three daughters of Raimon II of Turena—now Turenne. Bertran de Born declared them to be the three most beautiful women on Earth—the sort of statement that does not get forgotten. She married Eble V of Ventadorn. Maria was praised by several of the troubadours, and the single biographical summary of her says that she was not only the most beautiful lady in the Limousin but the most highly esteemed, the one who did most good and kept herself most thoroughly from evil (whatever that may be taken to mean). There is an unverified story that Uc de Saint-Circ, who is credited with the lines about her, had known Maria's brother. What use that may have been to him can scarcely be guessed. His relations with Raimon III of Turenne were acrimonious, as we know from the two surviving verse exchanges between them.

The poem she wrote as an exchange of verses with Gui d'Ussel probably dates from the last years of the twelfth century, near the time when the family of Ventadorn, Eble IV and his son, repelled an attempt by Richard Coeur de Lion to take the castle, after Richard's return from Acre and the Third Crusade, and after he wrote his *Chanson* as a prisoner of the emperor. Richard had hoped to be able to use Ventadorn as his own base in the Limousin.

Maria had a court at Ventadorn that welcomed and encouraged poets, in the tradition of Eble II. Gui d'Ussel had taken holy orders, but then for a time considered getting married. Then he decided that it was better to be a lover, whereupon the lady with whose future he had been trifling left him and mar ried someone else, and Gui was thrown into despair, which became common knowledge. He had stopped writing. In his songs he had praised not only the women he had been courting, but Maria "more than anyone," and she begins the dialogue:

Gui d'Ussel, I am grieved at you
because you are no longer singing,
and I hope that you still want to
because you understand such things.

And he replies to her question, which is whether a lady should do as much for a lover, if she courts him, as he does for her.

This one poem, half of it by someone else, reveals a woman with a strong, independent mind, self-assured and highly gifted. It is also an index of the freedom that had evolved in the Limousin courts in a few decades, and had survived Henry II's wreckage of Aliénor's court at Poitiers. But it cannot have been long after the poem was written that a papal legate demanded that Gui d'Ussel take a vow not to write any more poems. D'Ussel did not dispute the interference. He had, after all, taken holy orders, however dubious his vocation, and he had no choice but to obey. The power of papal legates in that time can be judged by their crucial role in the unleashing of the Albigensian Crusade, the elaborately vindictive public humiliation of the house of Toulouse, and the inauguration of the Inquisition. The church's attitude toward the activities and tradition, and the freedom of spirit, of the troubadours was never in doubt.

By the time that Philip Augustus, King of France, loosed the war machines and the plundering rabble of the Albigensian

Crusade, in 1209, against the Cathar "heretics" and the recalcitrant splendor of the civilization of the south, the great days of the troubadours were over at Ventadorn, and indeed the whole troubadour tradition and the code of courtly love would never be the same.

CHAPTER TEN

Bernart and the troubadours had brought me to Ventadour, but inevitably I became interested in the history of the château itself. In the middle years of the twentieth century a canon from Égletons, Léon Billet, devoted years of painstaking research to the history of the château and its heirs, and to Bernart and the troubadours of the region, with the patience of a builder of models. From his accounts I learned that in the fourteenth century a squire of the lord of Ventadour (as it had come to be called in the time) betrayed him and, for a sum of money, allowed the castle to fall into the hands of a large, ruthless band of robbers, who held it for over ten years, plundering the countryside, until they were outwitted in turn, and the leaders executed, and the castle returned to its owners. Froissart, the great fourteenth century chronicler of medieval France, was captivated by the story and devoted many pages to a detailed account of it that reads like a fairy tale.

The full architectural splendor of Ventadour came after that. All through the fifteenth century, the castle's heirs, generation by generation, rebuilt the massive circular tower of the château, with walls eleven feet thick at the base, and a slate roof. They added elegant stonework, tall curved doorways, the entrance portal of the main hall, a broad staircase, halls, galleries, bas-reliefs. They continued the additions and adornments of the château into the sixteenth century, rebuilding the present vaulted entrance, above which the panel with the relief of Samson killing the lion greeted all arrivals. Vast new ramparts and an outer ring of walls were erected, in some places rising seventy feet from the cliff at their base.

But during the sixteenth century the family spent less and less time at Ventadour, and at last moved to a town house in Ussel. Their ties to Ventadour frayed, and though they kept their complement of retainers there, the references to the sale of "debris from the château" date from years before the French Revolution.

After Ignace Perthuis du Roussillon et du Gay (who had managed to include in his ornate name many of the social and psychic incongruities of his historic moment) had given up ransacking the château, and had retired, still in debt, from the dilapidated scene, records were filed in *mairies* and in parish registers, but for the most part we are left to imagine the pillaged ruins passing through the latter years of French romanticism, the clouds of the nineteenth century sailing over the jagged walls and the woods closing around them. That corner of the

Languedoc sank deeper year by year into its own sleeping forest. The cutting and construction of the railroad from Brive to Tulle and Clermont, in the latter decades of the century, must have been an immense traumatic incision into a way of life that had come to seem changeless. Even when the tracks reached Égletons, and the station was built there, Moustier-Ventadour and the villages around it remained part of an apparently untouched age, an immemorial backwater, in which Appel and Smith came looking for the homes of the troubadours.

My wife and I went back to Ventadour in the autumn. Luc de Goustine showed us the inside of the church, and led us through the ruins of the château telling us the history of each section of the walls and of the attempts at restoration. More clearing had been done during the summer, along the steep slopes below the château. We clambered down the precipitous hillside, through the cut brush, to see Ventadour from below.

We found that the spur on which the castle was built was veined with quartz, and that we were making our way through a summer's growth of oaks, hazel, broom, yarrow, wild strawberry. And young hawthorns that must have germinated that spring, a handful within call. As we bent over them we could hear the torrents of the Soudeillette and the Vigne, the "moats of Ventadour" below us, and when we looked up we saw again the silent walls where the songs had begun.

EPILOGUE

After the age of Eble the Singer, and the days of Bernart de Ventadorn and of his successors in the family, those troubadours known as the "Four from Ussel" (Maria de Ventadorn and Gui d'Ussel were two of them), Eble's heirs upheld the family honor with distinction in military and diplomatic posts and in the church, until the French Revolution. The last of the senior line of descendants was the celebrated and popular Duke of Enghien, who was implicated in a royalist plot against Napoléon, and Bonaparte had him arrested even though he was not in France, and saw to it that he was shot in prison. The duke was thirty-two at the time, admired by many, and his fate was one of countless examples of the shabby vindictiveness that underlay Napoléon's great act.

From Léon Billet's research of the history of the château and church, and the surrounding country, and Bernart and the

"Four from Ussel," I learned that the family had not died out with the execution of the Duke of Enghien, but that a junior line had continued into the twentieth century. I approached the latter part of the family chronicle with misgivings, remembering things I had read and heard about some of the ancient families of France after Pétain's understanding with the Nazis in 1940, and the establishment of the Vichy government. Accounts of upper-class collaboration and proto-Fascism have continued to surface ever since the war: attitudes and behavior such as those depicted in Max Ophuls's film *The Sorrow and the Pity.*

During World War I the head of the d'Ussel family was François-Marie-Jacques d'Ussel, born in Paris in 1875. I felt a measure of reassurance as I read about him: a man of ascetic piety and dry probity, who fully expected to die in the battles of World War I, and wrote letters from the front vibrant with an exemplary stoicism and elevated patriotism, somewhat in the manner of Charles de Gaulle, years later. He survived the war and died on December 7, 1941, the day of the Japanese attack on Pearl Harbor and the American entry into World War II.

His son and heir was Guillaume, born in 1906. There is a picture of him as a child, running through the grass with the sun shining through his blond curly hair, in front of the family house at Neuvic, near Ventadour, years before the first war and his father's departure to write those noble letters.

After World War I, Guillaume attended the military academy at Saint-Cyr. Besides his father's immediate example, one of his uncles, Maréchal Lyautey, was a famous general. Guillaume distinguished himself, from the beginning, and as a young officer was officially described as "the finest tank officer in our army....From 1935 on, an exemplary commander of the tanks of the First Light Armored Division."

In May 1940, at the time of the Nazi invasion, he fought the Germans in Belgium and the north of France, from May 10 until the 23rd, when he was wounded at Mareuil. He was evacuated, cited for bravery and, after the fall of France, reassigned to a post as a military instructor. When the Vichy government was established and the military academy was moved to Aix, the French Army still existed, and he was offered the command of the first tank regiment, but refused it. When the army was disbanded in November of 1942, he went home to Neuvic.

He made contact at once with the French Resistance and offered his services.

The history of the Resistance in southwest France has emerged gradually through the decades since the liberation. François David, a history professor from Brive, spent years interviewing survivors and sifting through such records as were to be found. The movement began during the period of stunned demoralization after the fall of Paris, the Nazi occupation of the north of France, the armistice of June 1940, and the formation of the Vichy government, in the following month. Even before de Gaulle's call to arms to the French people, Edmond Michelet, in the southwest, had begun to assemble a corps of those who were prepared to risk everything in order to oppose the Germans.

The movement included Catholics and Communists working together. Some of the first published statements against the Vichy government and the German presence in France came from Catholics, officials of the church. Michelet's initial appeal invoked Charles Péguy, and a number of priests in the region had openly denounced Nazism and official collaboration with it. They were joined by political representatives of the left, and Freemasons. Among the first things they did was to provide shelter and care to refugees from the north, through the summer of 1940, an undertaking that led to the addition to their own ranks of determined and experienced opponents of the Nazis from among the refugees. They organized escape routes for Jewish refugees, escaped prisoners, English airmen shot down over France. Within a remarkably short time they had set up a network connecting the Auvergne and the Spanish border. Presbyteries, religious residences such as that of the Franciscan Fathers at St. Anthony's in Brive, priests' houses such as that of Father Léon Bédrune, took in refugees, anti-Nazi activists, Jews, and also hid arms. The nascent secret organization rapidly found assistants able to prepare false identity papers essential for many operations. In 1942 a number of explosions rocked the houses of several well-known collaborators with the Germans, in Brive. The Resistance had managed to set them off as warnings, and to do so without causing loss of life.

On November 11, 1942, when the German Army pushed south across the border with Vichy France and occupied the rest of the country, the Gestapo and the Vichy police began to work together to stamp out the by then well-established Resistance. It was at this point that Guillaume d'Ussel entered the organization.

Its leaders were of course delighted to be approached by a regular officer with such experience and of such proven ability. He was put in charge of the Organisation de la Résistance Armée for the region, which included, at that time, four *départe-*

ments. He took the code name Nicouleau. A few weeks later, in January, and again in February 1943, the Gestapo and the Vichy police in Tulle and Brive arrested nine of the principal organizers of the Resistance in the Corrèze, three of whom would not survive their imprisonment.

The activities of the Resistance and the Armée Secrète intensified during the next year and a half, as the fortunes of war turned against the Germans and both sides watched the progress of the Allies in Italy and waited for the invasion, which they became increasingly certain was coming from England. Besides the escape network, and the periodical, carefully planned assassinations of German officials, the Resistance was building up supplies of arms and essential combat materials in readiness for the day when concerted guerrilla operations could be carried out against the German forces. Within the Resistance the risks grew greater as the German occupants felt the increasing precariousness of their situation.

It was May again, the spring of 1944. Speculation about the coming invasion was a constant theme everywhere. Guillaume d'Ussel and two other officers of the Resistance were in Brive on a mission to Jean Moulin, whose office was on a boulevard then named for Maréchal Pétain (since renamed). As they left the office with Moulin, for a rendezvous with another Resistance leader a few streets away, a car full of Gestapo officers pulled up and stopped them, and took them to the Hôtel de Bordeaux. It seems possible that it was a routine investigation of a group of men who looked suspicious to the Germans, rather than the result of a tip-off. One of the group, Joubert, a young officer from the last class that had graduated from Saint-Cyr, was wearing a military raincoat and carrying a knapsack full of clothes destined for members of the Resistance who were then in hiding.

The Germans did not know who they had arrested. Their papers, false or authentic, were in order. But Moulin had given d'Ussel a list of parachute drops from Allied planes that were planned for the new moon in May, and at the moment of his arrest he had not managed to hide it satisfactorily. The men were searched. D'Ussel looked for some way to destroy or get rid of the list. Moulin wrote later that d'Ussel managed to edge over to a table on which one of the Gestapo agents had laid a briefcase, and he slipped the list under the briefcase. One of the police saw him do it and told the others, and the suspicions of the Gestapo were confirmed, although they still did not know who they had picked up.

The men were taken to the train station, and to Tulle for "questioning." None of them divulged information either at Brive or Tulle, and they were taken on to Limoges. In the meantime the news of their arrest had reached members of some of their families. The Germans evidently let such information out in the hopes of bringing about the kind of thing that, in this case, happened. The mother of the youngest of those arrested lost her head, rushed to the Germans, and, in a misguided attempt to save her son, told them that it was all Nicouleau's fault, and that he was really d'Ussel, for whom she knew they had been searching. D'Ussel had been trying to get the Germans to believe that he had been—that they had all been—arrested by mistake, but when confronted with this exposure he gave up the attempt.

D'Ussel was asked to disclose the names of those in his

clandestine organization.

"I am a French officer," he said. "I have given my word to my comrades in arms. I will tell you no names at all."

The interrogation continued. At one point d'Ussel asked his questioner, "Are you French or German?"

"German."

"I think rather better of you then. I was afraid you were French."

In the course of questioning an officer asked him, "Why have you joined the Resistance?"

"You cannot win this war. I have no doubt of that. It seems natural that I should want to prevent you from further harming my country, and that I should try to help those who are preparing to save us from you."

A French captain there, who was collaborating with the Germans, reproached him for joining the Resistance and encouraging young people to be part of it. D'Ussel stood up and said to him, "Sir, I have nothing to learn about courage from you. I refer you to my military record."

He was asked about the date when the Allied landing was to take place. "I know nothing about that," he said. "Military secrets of that kind are not relayed to me, fortunately."

A Frenchman in Gestapo uniform said to him, "So you are one of those who imagine that one fine morning the radio will announce an Allied invasion of the French coast. Forget it. I know your English friends. I saw how they cleared out at Dunkerque. They're a bunch of bums. If I managed to get onto a boat myself it was no thanks to them."

"Maybe," d'Ussel said to him. "But if you are alive and well and walking around today you owe it to my tanks which fought to the last to cover your retreat. This is the reward for that."

According to Sordet, one of the others arrested that day, the reply produced an uneasy hush in the room, and the German captain brought the session to a close.

D'Ussel was tortured during the interrogations then and later, but never told the Germans anything. He and his companions were sent to a prison in Limoges, and there they learned of the Allied landings in Normandy. The prisoners nursed a hope of being liberated soon, but instead they were loaded onto a train, destination undisclosed. They learned that other sections of the train were carrying a German armored division. They stopped at a large station which they recognized as Poitiers, and there they came under heavy aerial bombardment. Their train seemed to be a principal target. There were 350 prisoners crowded together and they piled up against each other, covering their heads with whatever they had. D'Ussel, they noticed, sat calmly through the whole thing. He was asked why he did not at least lie down. He said that the risk was the same lying down as sitting up, "and if my hour was up, the bombs would have got me just the same." Asked then whether he was not afraid of dying, he answered that he was Catholic and believed in eternal life.

The armored division that had been the object of the bombing was the 2nd SS Panzer Division, "Das Reich," one of the most loathed units of the Wehrmacht. In that same May of 1944, as the Germans began to withdraw from the south of France in anticipation of the Normandy landings, they did so with a bitter vengefulness which they visited upon the region they had occupied with such small success. South of the Corrèze,

German units, many of them from SS divisions, made special detours to remote hamlets, to massacre defenseless country people. On the upland south of Gramat a patrol left the main road, followed a small lane to an intersection in the woods where there was a cluster of farm buildings, forced all the inhabitants out into a small clearing. There were a few dozen old men and women, and children. The Germans lined them up and shot them all, then shut the barn doors and set fire to the buildings with animals inside. The Reich division left a particularly gruesome wake. In Tulle it took out ninety-nine men associated by rumor if nothing else with the Resistance, and hanged them along the main street, in full view of their friends and families. Farther north, at Oradour-sur-Glane, they herded 642 residents, many of them women and children, into the church, locked the doors, and set the building alight.

With rumors of the Allied advance in the north filtering through to them, d'Ussel and some of his companions traveled on to Compiègne, then to Dachau. On the journey to Dachau 963 prisoners died on the train.

One of d'Ussel's fellow prisoners at the camp there was André Delpech, a nineteen-year-old from the Lot, who had been in the Resistance in Toulouse. The Germans had classified everyone alphabetically. Delpech was close to d'Ussel. He got to observe the captain at close quarters, and he was impressed then and in retrospect by his unbroken dignity.

D'Ussel's character impressed the *kapos* in the camp too, and they resented it and deliberately made things worse for him. Delpech and d'Ussel found themselves working side by side. At one point they were digging underground galleries for a

Mercedes factory. Then for two weeks they worked digging a tunnel by a Nazi watchtower, a bomb shelter, perhaps. "Even in such absurd drudgery," Delpech said, "in spite of hunger, lice, humiliations, he kept the same dignity of manner and faced it all with the same nobility. I saw that if these men who were products of the Nazis were intent upon humiliating him, the dignity of his own attitude raised him far above their bullying and violence. They certainly hurt him in every way they could, but in the end even they realized that they were abusing a human being who was quite superior to them."

The two men were separated, and then met again in the prison block of the camp at Neckargerach, in November 1944, two years after d'Ussel had joined the Resistance. Delpech found him a few minutes before his death there on November 27, 1944, from exhaustion and dysentery.

D'Ussel was awarded the Cross of the Légion d'Honneur posthumously. His son still lives, part of the year, in the family house at Neuvic, not far from the ruins at Ventadour.

I learned that the house in the village, at the corner, with the *Antiquitiés* sign and the lace curtains, had been a kind of unofficial club, a meeting place for those in the know locally and in the region, for decades after the war, and the lady whom we had seen watching us when we first drove past was known far and wide.

During those same years, another lady who lived in the neighborhood, and was associated with the heirs of Ventadour, had kept garden furniture in one of the ruined towers of the château and had given garden parties in the great courtyards, and the parties too, for a while, acquired legends. I imagine the summer hats, the chairs overlooking the valleys.

Since 1963, the excavation, reclamation, and partial restoration of the remains of the ancient walls has proceeded slowly, with the encouragement of the Lévis-Mirepoix family (the Marquis of Lévis-Mirepoix bought the château in 1895) and the assistance of the business concerns in the area. As with many projects of the kind, it is not entirely clear what can really be put back, or should be. A rather flimsy, anomalous wire fence and gate now protect what remains of the great citadel, but what the walls themselves once fostered and heard has gone everywhere.

ABOUT THE AUTHOR

W. S. MERWIN is the author of more than fifteen volumes of poetry, including *The River Sound* and *The Vixen*. The recipient of the Pulitzer Prize, the Bollingen Prize, and the Tanning Prize for mastery in the art of poetry, he has also written numerous plays and prose books, including *The Lost Upland*, a memoir of life in the south of France. Merwin lives and works in Maui, Hawaii, where he maintains a garden of rare palm trees.

This book is set in Garamond 3, designed by
Morris Fuller Benton and Thomas Maitland
Cleland in the 1930s, and Monotype Grotesque,
both released digitally by Adobe.

Printed by R. R. Donnelley and Sons on
Gladfelter 60-pound Thor Offset smooth
white antique paper.

Dust jacket printed by Miken Companies.
Color separation by Quad Graphics.

Three-piece case of Ecological Fiber cardinal side
panels with Sierra black book cloth as the spine
fabric. Stamped in Lustrofoil metallic silver.